ALSO BY CHERYL MENDELSON

Home Comforts

Morningside Heights

Love, Work, Children

Anything for Jane

The Good Life

VOWS

The Modern Genius
of an Ancient Rite

Cheryl Mendelson

SIMON & SCHUSTER
New York   Toronto   London   Sydney   New Delhi

1230 Avenue of the Americas
New York, NY 10020

First Simon & Schuster hardcover edition May 2024

SIMON & SCHUSTER and colophon are registered trademarks of Simon & Schuster, LLC

Simon & Schuster: Celebrating 100 Years of Publishing in 2024

For information about special discounts for bulk purchases, please contact Simon & Schuster Special Sales at 1-866-506-1949 or business@simonandschuster.com.

The Simon & Schuster Speakers Bureau can bring authors to your live event. For more information or to book an event, contact the Simon & Schuster Speakers Bureau at 1-866-248-3049 or visit our website at www.simonspeakers.com.

Interior design by Wendy Blum

Manufactured in the United States of America

1   3   5   7   9   10   8   6   4   2

Library of Congress Cataloging-in-Publication Data
Names: Mendelson, Cheryl, 1946– author.
Title: Vows : the modern genius of an ancient rite / Cheryl Mendelson.
Description: First Simon & Schuster hardcover edition. | New York : Simon & Schuster, [2024] | Includes bibliographical references and index.
Identifiers: LCCN 2023052887 (print) | LCCN 2023052888 (ebook) | ISBN 9781668021569 (hardcover) | ISBN 9781668021576 (trade paperback) | ISBN 9781668021583 (ebook)
Subjects: LCSH: Marriage customs and rites. | Vows. | Marriage.
Classification: LCC GT2665 .M46 2024 (print) | LCC GT2665 (ebook) | DDC 203/.85–dc23/eng/20231122
LC record available at https://lccn.loc.gov/2023052887
LC ebook record available at https://lccn.loc.gov/2023052888

ISBN 978-1-6680-2156-9
ISBN 978-1-6680-2158-3 (ebook)

For E

CONTENTS

CONTENTS

APPENDIXES

[M]arriage, the *only* subject.

—W. H. Auden, letter to James Stern, October 1944

Mayor: We are gathered together here in the presence of these witnesses to join this man and this woman in matrimony, which is an honorable estate, and is not to be entered into unadvisedly or lightly, but reverently and discreetly . . .

Mayor to the Groom: _____, will you take this woman to be your wedded wife, to live together in the estate of matrimony? Will you love, honor and keep her; in sickness and in health, and forsaking all others, keep yourself only unto her, as long as you both shall live?

Mayor to the Bride: _____, will you take this man to be your wedded husband, to live together in the estate of matrimony? Will you love, honor and keep him; in sickness and in health, and forsaking all others, keep yourself only unto him, so long as you both shall live?

Mayor to the Groom: _____, take _____ by the hand and repeat after me. "I, _____, take thee _____, to be my wedded wife, to have and to hold from this day forward, for better, for worse, for richer, for poorer, in sickness and in health, to love and to cherish until death do us part."

Mayor to the Bride: _____, repeat after me. "I, _____, take thee _____, to be my wedded husband, to have and to hold from this day forward, for better, for worse, for richer, for poorer, in sickness and in health, to love and to cherish, until death do us part."

Mayor: For as much as _____ and _____ have consented together in wedlock and have witnessed the same before this company, and thereto have given and pledged their troth, each to the other, and have declared the same by joining hands.

Now, by the authority vested in me by the State of Michigan and the Office of Mayor of the City of _____, I pronounce you to be husband and wife and extend to you my best wishes for a successful and happy married life together.

—The Civil Marriage Ceremony Handbook for Mayors of Michigan (2015)

I

Foundations

Chapter One

MY *TROTH*?

So I, admiring of his qualities:
Things base and vile, holding no quantity,
Love can transpose to form and dignity:
Love looks not with the eyes, but with the mind;
And therefore is wing'd Cupid painted blind.

—William Shakespeare, *A Midsummer Night's Dream*, Act 1, Scene 1

My interest in the marriage vows first sparked when I found myself unexpectedly taking them. It was a tragicomic experience.

The man I was marrying had been my college boyfriend. But soon after graduation, when we were fledgling graduate students at different universities, he announced that he thought we should date other people while continuing as lovers in an intimate partnership. I couldn't do that. We broke up, at least theoretically, but teary telephone calls continued for weeks. In a state of indescribable misery, I withdrew from the university and made plans to go stay with friends in Boston and look for a job. En route, I would stop to say goodbye in person. This, we thought, would make the break real and final, but I never made it to Boston.

We spent three days breaking up. To my surprise—I had thought he'd be relieved—as I packed up to go to the airport, he became increasingly upset and finally fell ill with a fierce attack of migraine. I knew he was prone to these excruciating headaches, but I hadn't ever seen him go through one, and I was shocked and worried. In the midst of his pain and nausea, he asked me to marry him. His agony paralyzed me with guilt. Worse, I interpreted this quagmire of guilt, pain, dependency, and need as frustrated mutual love. Marriage would fix it. I said yes. We decided to do it immediately and planned to go for a license the next day.

But first we called our parents. All four of them were aghast at what was obviously impulsive, irrational behavior and tried hard to talk us out of it. His finally hung up on us. Mine were more determined. "Don't do anything until we get there," my father shouted. They drove a thousand miles and showed up the following night with my baby brother.

The next day, the legal waiting period having ended, we climbed the steps of city hall, where a judge in black robes awaited us. My mother was resigned but my father was still trying to talk me out of it. "No one's going to laugh at you if you back out now," he said. "It's not too late." I was insulted—as though I would actually marry someone because I was afraid of being laughed at! Meanwhile, my soon-to-be-husband was now over his migraine and looking stony-faced, but he didn't suggest calling it off. The five of us entered the judge's chambers, grim and nervous.

The gray-haired judge took in this disgruntled family group

with a frown—the despairing parents; the confused and worried four-year-old who couldn't figure out why the grown-ups were upset; the now openly angry young groom in an ill-fitting suit bought that morning at my father's insistence, down the block from a jewelry store where we found a cheap gold ring. Gently, the judge asked a few questions, trying to warm things up. He sighed and opened a black book, explaining, to my surprise, that we were to say "I will," not "I do," when he put questions to us. Then he read out a wedding ceremony filled with ancient rhythms and words foreign to my Appalachian Presbyterian ears, archaic versions of the marriage vows about loving and honoring each other, for better, for worse, for richer, for poorer, in sickness and in health, and forsaking all others, as long as we both lived, and thereto pledging our *troth*. (I now know this to have been an American version of the 1662 Anglican ceremony.)

The groom choked out his "I will"s, but when the troth business came up, he interrupted to ask, in a snidely bright conversational tone, "What's a troth?" The judge only paused to give him a cold stare and went on with the ceremony. Horribly embarrassed, I saw that I should put a stop to the whole thing, but I still had some idea that the only way out of our tangle was forward. Once we were married, all this pain, guilt, shame, and madness would be cured by the power of the institution. Also, I did see with terrible clarity how everyone *would* laugh if I backed out now. The story would be repeated by my siblings with howls of hilarity at every Thanksgiving dinner, forever. This, obviously, was no reason to go through with it, but it raised in me some perverse, defiant wish to do the wrong thing. I plunged. As the judge closed his black book, he turned to my new husband and told him, in an icy voice that he probably had only ever used to address convicted murderers, that "troth" meant truth and faithfulness.

Was I less mature than the average twenty-two-year-old? I can only hope so. We had what I came to call a hysterical marriage, licensed but not really a marriage—like a hysterical pregnancy, when the woman swells but not with a baby. We had the certificate but not the reality—not for a moment. My always angry husband was soon spouting sarcastic criticism not only of his own marriage but of all marriages. A surprising number of our friends shared his views. In our graduate-student social world the dominant attitude toward matrimony was negative, even contemptuous. In a way, it allowed our promises no legitimacy. Adultery was commonplace. Other people came on to both of us, in his case successfully, which led to repeated separations and increasingly tense reunions. After seven years, we parted permanently.

It's hard to imagine a world in which our absurd decision to marry wouldn't have ended in divorce. But I could see that friends whose marriages had more propitious beginnings than ours had to fight many of the same battles. The general atmosphere of suspicion toward the institution seemed to me to seep into actual marriages, exaggerating their frustrations and minimizing their satisfactions. Most marriages in our circle of friends broke up. Social hostility toward marriage and even toward love, expressed in contempt, disapproval, and unfriendly theorizing, took a toll on both.

The tracks of this miserable marital experience are all over this book. It's preoccupied with the vows and their history, how love works, how couples and their social worlds interact, how unfriendly social surroundings affect couples, how different social practices and institutions erected to deal with love have profound political and economic effects.

Many truths about love and marriage tend to be overlooked and underthought because they lie on unclaimed turf. They are a subject that belongs to the world of values and the subjective parts of life—to religion or ethics, perhaps, but to no field of scientific expertise. Historians, social scientists, biologists, and economists have no techniques to lay bare its secrets. If they have to deal with it, they mostly talk around it, eyes averted, or they circle it warily, preferring indirect approaches, for example in theories about divorce or marriage rates or sexual behaviors. Psychologists and psychoanalysts, clerics, and professional moralists do claim the subject and say important things about it, but, historians of church liturgies aside, they are mostly silent about its ceremonies and rituals and how they reflect and shape the interactions of couples, love, and social relations. This book explores a patch of this abandoned ground.

In some ways, marriage is a historical constant, a social form that holds its shape through human revolutions because that shape answers to underlying, unchanging human realities. Human revolutions, however, have been frequent in the past sixty years, and the laws of marriage have changed dramatically. In 1967 the United States Supreme Court, in *Loving v. Virginia*, held that the many state laws banning interracial marriage were unconstitutional. Soon after *Loving*, no-fault divorce laws were enacted in every state, and the following years also saw scores of narrower changes in most states' laws, many of them directed toward making men and women equal under the law. In 2015, *Obergefell v. Hodges* established constitutional protection for same-sex marriage. Some people press for further changes, whether to make marriage conform to new social and political values or to overturn revolutions of the past half century.

This means that to write about the marriage vows—which in some respects predate these revolutions by nearly a millennium—is to pick one's way through a cultural minefield. Whether wedding vows need rethinking, updating, or, possibly, discarding is now a wide-open question. Having thought, read, and rethought, I concluded—for reasons that this book exists to lay out—that the answer is a solid *no*. The traditional marriage vows, though they contain phrases composed a thousand or more years ago, are a form of words that say exactly what love still wants to say. Over the centuries, particular words and specific vows have come and gone, but the modern versions all retain ancient cadences and phrases. Even the most recent change, which dropped the woman's vow of obedience, is at least a century old. Deleting that vow was, moreover, merely a return to the rite's origins, for the oldest vows on record were simple, identical promises for men and women.

The medieval promises included in the modern versions are startlingly free of offenses to modern sensibilities. They don't create social, racial, cultural, classist, or sexual exclusions, and they don't erect hierarchies and inequalities of any sort. They easily embrace gay marriage without a single altered word because they are about a certain kind of love—marital love. Morally, formal marriage is freely available to any two people who share that kind of love, whose nature is a subject of this book. Legally, you can get married without love, but marriage is more than a legal status. Wedding vows exist to honor and protect marital love.

Ceremonies based on vows, for obvious reasons, do not work for nonconsensual systems of matrimony. To vow is to bind oneself, by one's words, to some action. If a "vow" is forced, it isn't self-binding—someone other than oneself commands it—and isn't really a vow. Vows thus have a natural fit with marriage based on love, which is never something done to you but something you yourself freely choose. Marriage for love can exist only where mate choice is free.

But around the world and throughout history, mate choice has not been free in a number of ways. Marriage by bride capture (sometimes ritualized, with the bride's advance consent) once existed on every continent—in Brazilian tribes, the Mayans, ancient and early medieval European peoples, Greenland natives, Tibetans, the Maori, Australian Indigenous peoples, the Chinese and Indians. Parents everywhere exercised powerful authority over their children's marriages, and in many regions preferred that their children marry their cousins—a policy still common in some parts of the world as it ensures solidarity among family clans and keeps dowry wealth within the clan. Mate choice was often based on clan, totem, tribe, or blood relationship. Of course, love can and does arise in such systems, but it must make heavy compromises with other motives. If unbendable rules dictate that a man must marry his mother's brother's daughter, he probably doesn't marry her for love or think of marriage as the means of satisfying love. When mates aren't freely chosen for love, the connection between love and marriage will be more tenuous.

In the Western world, two thousand and more years ago, a limited type of monogamy was the law in ancient Greece and Rome. Men were permitted to have only one legal wife, who held all marital legal privileges, but men (not, of course, women) might also have additional relationships with concubines and sexual relations with women of lower social orders and with slaves. Nor was marriage open to all comers. Throughout the first millennium, in Rome and much of Christianized Europe, slaves could not marry each other, and free people could not marry slaves. The marriage of a Roman senator, or his son or grandson, to a freed woman or an actress was void. (Acting was not considered a respectable profession.) In feudal Europe, too, a nobleman and a lower-class woman could have only a limited type of marriage in which the woman and their children had no inheritance rights, but the children were legitimate, not bastardized. Serfs needed their lords' permission to marry. Household servants, apprentices, and laborers might not marry without their masters' permission.

The church always called for monogamy, but throughout the first millennium it regarded matrimony as a secular matter to be left to civil authorities. In England, only late in the eleventh century did the church gain control over marriage law. Over the centuries, the church increasingly supported freedom of choice in mates and even took steps toward backing children's right to defy parental control over their marriages. (Remember the helpful friar in *Romeo and Juliet*.) But, while eventually favoring individual choice in choosing a mate, it instituted a very strict form of monogamy. It forbade divorce. Married people who separated could not marry someone else until one of them died. In the long run, the church's success in forwarding monogamy resulted in vast improvements in women's status and condition and, indirectly, led to a broader social equality and, eventually, sexual equality, a story revisited in later sections of this book. The Reformation widely resecularized marriage but retained its monogamy and its vows, which were supported in Protestantism both by religious instruction and also via the spirit of individual self-determination that the Reformation fostered. Vows seemed the natural way for self-governing people to tie themselves together with bonds of love.

In the West, marrying is now so thoroughly identified with ceremonial vow-taking that "taking vows" is a synonym for getting married. It's a surprise to realize that this custom is actually a historical and anthropological oddity. Most of the world, for most of history, married without vows. Edward Westermarck's three-volume *History of Human Marriage* reports no wedding vows outside the West. Traditional weddings among native peoples of Asia, Africa, Australia, and the Americas had and have no vow-taking. Vows—solemn promises—are important in many societies, and were important in the ancient world, but they weren't part of weddings. In ancient Rome, the only promises relating to marriage were spelled out in a contract between the father of the bride and the groom or his father that laid out mostly financial terms, including questions of dowry, support, and penalties for misbehavior. The bride was not party to the contract, and she and the groom made no vows to each other. The wedding celebrations of Islam, Judaism, Hinduism, Shintoism, and the Eastern Orthodox Church are lovely, but traditionally included no vows. Buddhism prescribes no wedding ceremony. Online, you can now read vows for all of these religions and philosophies, but they are recent additions.

In modern times, Western-style monogamy spread throughout the world in a remarkably short period, and the popular rite of vows spread with it. In the late nineteenth century, weddings in Asia, Africa, and elsewhere began to include ceremonies in which couples took vows of love and fidelity "for better for worse," and so on. Today you'll see it in Seoul, Hong Kong, and Kuala Lumpur. In Japan, a majority of marriages include those same vows along with other Western elements, either alone or mixed with more traditional Shinto rituals. In Africa, many young couples take the vows at weddings with a white bridal gown, a walk down the aisle, and other common elements of the Western wedding—often combined with local rituals.

In some cases, Westernized marriage follows the adoption of Western religion, but in others, as in Japan, a secular version of the wedding rite was adopted and religion is ignored. Throughout the West, too, the traditional vows, scrubbed of religious content and context, are just as likely to be matter-of-factly read out by mayors, judges, and registrars in civil ceremonies as by clerics in churches. This development brings history full circle, back to marriage as the secular and civil event it was until about a thousand years ago.

Marriage by vow presupposes free choice, and free choice makes love matches possible. This is why marriage for love and marriage by vow develop together. The history of marriage by vow tracks a thousand-year transformation of marriage in which the obligations of marriage became a matter of self-imposed law and hence of freedom; the weight of kin, clan, custom, money, and power decreased and that of love and freedom increased; and female subordination ended and sexual equality began. The marriage vows evolved in one small region of the West that also, eventually, gave birth to the world's sturdiest democracies. Marriage by vow, egalitarian and democratic ideals, and marriage for love all grew up together, as mutually reinforcing ideals. The global popularity of Western-style marriage and its wedding rite reflects the spread of these values—freedom, love, and equality—throughout the world. Wherever they travel, they support the best hope for personal happiness and social good that the world has ever come up with.

Chapter Two

PROMISES

Unlike most secular promises, in principle, if not invariably in fact, the marriage vow is unique; it forms a bond that (ideally) cannot be undone other than by death.

—Herbert J. Schlesinger, *Promises, Oaths, and Vows:*
On the Psychology of Promising (2008)

No one can promise to suspend gravity or make the Mississippi flow northward. Can anyone promise to love—forever? In the belief that love and the distant future are equally out of their control, many couples abandon the traditional marriage vows or forgo marriage altogether. They point to the divorce rate, the prevalence of adultery, and the number of loveless and miserable marriages that began with sincere, solemn vows of undying love, and they conclude that the marriage vows are a sweet but meaningless archaism—a bow to tradition for its own sake, which does next to nothing for marriages. They write their own affectionate, touching, or funny speeches that don't promise but sincerely *hope* for lifelong love and fidelity.

Yet anyone who has ever been in love knows that love demands and bestows promises. If you've ever made a serious declaration of love, you probably don't doubt that it amounts to a lot more than stating an interesting fact about your feelings. The lover invites—*wants*—the loved person to rely on their exclusive, tender, sexual regard. A declaration of love *is*, in fact, a promise, even if "promise" never gets said. To declare love is to promise affection, loyalty, protection, erotic appreciation, and much more, and to ask for a return. It's a bid to get into a forever relationship: love never wants to end. It creates bonds, ties, and expectations. Once love is declared, infidelity and betrayal are possible, which is why some people refuse to say "I love you" even when they do. They know that words of love make a promise.

Promises, not love, are the subject at hand, but the two get tangled together in several ways. People whose promises are unreliable are likely to be unreliable in love. The ability to love rests on character qualities that also support the ability to promise. A social world in which promises are weak is a society in which love is weak. In our era, promises are weak, but they need not be. Nor should we shrug this off—not if we want to hold on to a world where everyone can hope for love.

To promise is to bind oneself to some future action and invite at least one person to rely on the promise, someone to whom the performance matters. Generally, promises are useful only in situations where there's some possibility that the promisor might have to perform the promise despite conflicting inclinations or wishes, or where the promisee might realistically fear such a possibility. This is why we *promise* to repay a loan, to be at the party—and to love you forever. A promise is called a *vow* when it is an especially serious promise. In some religious traditions, a promise constitutes a vow only if it is made to God, but in this book a vow is simply a solemn promise.

Promises Then and Now

Anyone who spends time with teenagers knows that among them promises are undervalued social capital. Teens may react to a request for a promise as a violation of their autonomy. If they promise to meet a friend for a shopping trip or a movie, that may mean only "If I feel like it then." Though they may use the word, they don't actually promise; they merely predict with a fair amount of confidence what they will want to do when the time comes. The obvious downside to this abandoning of promises is that they can't be sure who, if anyone, will come to their party. They don't know until they are standing in front of the theater whether they have a date for the movie. Their secret may or may not be kept.

In a long historical trend, we in the twenty-first century make less use of vows and promises, and have less confidence in them, than our ancestors. In contemporary film and fiction, promises rarely serve any dramatic purpose except to illustrate faithlessness. The merest hint that a promise is serious and solemn means that it's going to be broken. It's unlikely that anyone today would write about characters who hold rigidly, insanely, or, above all, *nobly* to their promises, yet these were frequent themes in drama and fiction from ancient times through the nineteenth century. The center of the action in George Meredith's 1879 novel, *The Egoist*, is Clara's promise to marry Sir Willoughby. She begs to be released from the promise, having discovered his egoism. He responds, "Bride is bride, and wife is wife, and affianced is, in honour, *wedded*. You cannot be released." For much of the book, she feels—irrationally, in the opinion of us readers—that unless he releases her, she must marry him. This, of course, renders her desperate, and the comedy is off and running, with more reminders for our times about how serious the solemn promise was in older days.

Daniel Donoghue, a professor of medieval literature, compares the promise-making of our day with that of a thousand years ago. He quotes a sermon by Archbishop Wulfstan (d. 1023) upbraiding his fellow Anglo-Saxons for their sins and crimes—murder, rape, mutilation, and more. Such terrible wrongs, however, are not their worst, Wulfstan says. What could be even worse than those crimes?

> [W]e know well where that wretched deed has happened that a father has sold his son for a price, and a son his mother, and one brother has sold another into the control of foreigners. And all these are great and terrible deeds, let him understand who will. And yet what harms this people is still greater and even more manifold . . . ; many are forsworn and greatly perjured . . . , and pledges . . . are broken again and again.

Promise-breaking and "forswearing" are what is worse. "Forswear," an English word that is all but dead, means to renounce or abandon an oath or promise.

As Donoghue points out, most people today think that breaking promises is nothing compared with the horror of selling your mother or son into slavery, but Wulfstan clearly says that promise-breaking and false swearing are the greater evils, in fact the worst ones. "[T]o Wulfstan the bond of the spoken word was the *only* glue that held society together," Donoghue explains. "His *Sermo* ends with several exhortations to 'keep carefully oath and pledge . . . and have some loyalty . . . between us without deceit.'"

In an introduction to a children's book back in the 1960s, the poet W. H. Auden makes the same point to explain to children the significance of the broken promise in the story of the Pied Piper. Like Donoghue, Auden wants his young readers to grasp the paramount importance of promises in the past compared to today:

> You, too, could tell the story [of the Pied Piper] about your home town. If you live in Manhattan, you could tell how the Piper arrived at City Hall, how he led the rats away to the Battery, and how—when the Mayor refused to pay him—he led all the children down into the I.R.T. subway station at Fourteenth Street, out of which they never appeared again. Of course, you would have to make the sum of money offered by the Mayor much bigger—a million dollars perhaps.
>
> If you were telling the story this way, you might suddenly think: "But why was the Piper such a fool? Why didn't he insist upon a written contract, signed by the Mayor and himself, and witnessed by a Notary Public? Then, if the Mayor refused to pay, the Piper could have taken him to Court. As soon as the Judge saw the contract, the Mayor would have had to pay or go to prison."
>
> Today, if somebody breaks a promise we despise him and don't want to be friends with him, but in the old days not

keeping one's word was a much more serious matter. When few people could read or write, most business deals were made by word of mouth. There were no regular police to enforce law and order, so peaceful life depended upon promises being kept. To break one's promise was regarded as the worst crime anybody could commit, far worse than murder.

The Psychology of Promising

Herbert J. Schlesinger, a psychoanalyst, wrote a book, *Promises, Oaths, and Vows* (2008), that sheds light on the social decline of promises. In his view, it's still true today that a society cannot function unless its people are able to make and keep promises and regard it as morally wrong to break a promise. Every promise, he points out, involves at least three parties—not only a promisor and a promisee, but also a witness. The witness, who may or may not be a human person and may be physically or symbolically present, represents the social authority that backs the promise. The ability to make a promise rests on the fact that the words "I promise" or "I swear" or "I vow" carry weight, and they carry weight only if the society in which they are uttered grants them weight.

When society doesn't back promises, promisors can't get promisees to trust them and promisees can't rely on the world to see that they have been wronged if their promisor breaches. The third-party witness represents the *social force* of the promise—the fact that not only this promisee but other people generally will hold a person to their word whether by light or informal sanctions (distrust, frowns, dislike), or serious ones (complete ostracism), or heavy, extreme ones (damages in a lawsuit or prison for major fraudsters). A serious or solemn promise is a little piece of social capital that can be squandered or saved. When politicians routinely break campaign promises, voters have no faith in the honest promises of a politician who really would make good on them. Broken promises by some people diminish the value not only of their own future promises but also of everyone else's promises. Apply these thoughts to the realm of love and marriage and you see how, in some important ways, today's lovers have a harder row to hoe than ever before in history.

In everyday life, in dealings with families, friends, and casual business contacts, the social demand to keep promises is witnessed mostly *internally*—by the promisor's own conscience, the internalized voice of the social moral demands. Someone may act on that internal social voice by promising "on my honor" or on my heart or soul or life—or they might say, as children used to, "cross my heart and hope to die." Shaking hands or placing the hand on the heart have the same force. The call on the witness shows that the words are more than a mere statement of present intent. This is important because there is a large gray area between announcing intentions and making true promises. A witness creates more confidence in the promise and more motivation to keep it. The witness, Schlesinger says, becomes "a helper to keep the promise, or . . . an enforcer of it." In the Middle Ages, when vassals swore fealty with their hands on a relic of the saints, the relic served to call on holy and divine witnesses to back this especially solemn promise.

Secret Promises

Promises of love are a dance the couple do with their world, and unless both partners to the dance know the steps, trips and falls are likely. If two people keep their relationship or engagement secret, the world cannot back it or respect it. Other people might bad-mouth one to the other or ask one out or fall in love with one or try to seduce one, or invite just one to a party, and so on. The situation gets tricky and creates social ambiguities that novelists like to write about.

A subplot in Jane Austen's *Emma* centers on the moral ambiguities of *private love*. The secret engagement between Frank and Jane leads to fibs, saying the wrong things to the wrong people, entertaining false hopes, and enormous stress. In *Sense and Sensibility*, Marianne and Willoughby behave with a mild impropriety and keep their relations secret and private. This convinces everyone that they're in love and secretly engaged—when they're not. Meanwhile, Marianne, too, thinks they are engaged, but their secrecy deprives her of social protection. Willoughby's eventual betrayal so devastates her that she falls ill and almost dies. Trust Austen to supply a happy ending—unlike Shakespeare. Having secretly married, Romeo and Juliet both die.

On formal occasions involving important promises, laws and customs today sometimes still demand the bodily presence of one or more witnesses. In courtrooms, when someone takes the stand and promises to tell the truth "so help me God," that promise is witnessed by the clerk of the court who "administers" the oath, the judge, jury, lawyers, parties, and onlookers. In daily life, too, you still occasionally hear someone say "as God is my witness" to shore up a promise or oath, and public offices may still require new officeholders to take an oath to uphold the standards of that office in a public ceremony—before a gathering of people, following a traditional ritual.

Many states require witnesses to be present at a couple's marriage. Custom expects a couple's friends, relatives, mentors, and often their coworkers and colleagues to attend their weddings, though few people now realize that they, too, are there to witness. Custom, and in some places law, calls for the marriage vows to be "heard" by an officiant. This would once have been an authority figure approved by statute to perform this function, a cleric or judge or the mayor—but no, not sea captains, though fiction sometimes delegates this authority to them. In recent years, an increasing number of weddings are officiated by a best friend or relative of the couple, who has been "ordained" only by the Universal Life Church online—one of many signs that marriage vows often are not taken as seriously as they once were. Today, two people who take marriage vows may well have no serious witness—no "helper to keep the promise"—and, socially speaking, the vows likely are featherweight.

I am reminded of an early quarrel in my first marriage, conducted in whispers on the stairs of a high floor of the library stacks. (We were immature but not inconsiderate; we respected libraries' quiet.) The quarrel ended with my dramatically pulling off my wedding ring and flinging it down the open, winding stairway, which was at least eight stories high. Then we made up and urgently searched the staircase for the ring. A student going up as we came down paused and, helpfully, bent over to look with us. "What are we looking for?" he asked. When we told him, "A wedding ring," he pulled up and said, "Sure you want to find it?" and climbed on. The message couldn't have been clearer. When the entire larger society gives all couples that message, they are all on their own, their word backed up only by their own consciences, and their consciences, too, meeting with a good deal of social indifference. Moral and emotional confusion are often the result.

Confusion also results from entirely personal causes. Promises are psychologically complicated. A promise is what philosophers call a "speech act" or a "performative utterance." How do you bind yourself to keep a secret? Simply by saying, "I promise I won't tell." Saying the word "promise" *makes* it a promise—like magic—like saying "abracadabra" and making a rabbit hop out of an empty hat. A promise exists close to the line between reality and fantasy, or between reality-oriented thinking and the kind of thinking that dominates in dreams and psychosis. This makes some people vulnerable, in promise-making, to confusions of word and deed, of thought and reality, and to infection by neuroticism. Their romantic and marital relations fall prey in familiar ways to their general problem with promising.

The most obvious cases of slightly crazy promises are the childish ones that some adults repeatedly make, then break. The spendthrift buyer, who has broken many promises to control their spending, sincerely promises anew, then sets out for the mall with their credit card smoldering in their wallet. False promises of this kind are perfectly sincere. The promisors want to inspire not only trust but approval for their good intentions, but they repeatedly fail to keep their word. Like small children, they act almost as though saying the words of promise is all that's needed, as though they think: If my word is my bond, then in speaking it I've done all that I need to do. They freely dispense promises, feel remorseful when they breach them, and then offer solemn assurances that "this time I really mean it." Some types of serial adulterers and alcoholics seem to fit this mold.

On the other side of the coin, there are people who insist on keeping promises even when doing so is a kind of madness— as though they had no power to undo the "magic" connection between word and deed. Something hardly short of madness appears in miserable marriages when one spouse insists on his or her wedding vows as forbidding divorce from a spouse guilty of repeated, serious misconduct, including murderous threats that are eventually carried out.

The most common kind of neurotic reaction to the promises of marriage, however, is the one that scores of books and agony aunts have made familiar. These bear a close affinity to another case described by Schlesinger. A stockbroker, after years of study and market experience, came up with an investment strategy that he wanted to try out in the market. He would have had to follow it to the letter to give it a real test, but every time he set out to do so, he found himself "impulsively" abandoning the strategy and doing something different, even though this defeated the purpose of testing it and almost invariably made him lose money. It turned out that he behaved the same way in other parts of his life. This man feared being "trapped by any plan, commitment, or promise he might make." He reacted even to his own plan as if it "would acquire a motive force external to him . . . Each decision and plan he made had in it the seeds of a potential compulsion, and, to protect himself, he had to defeat his own plan before it defeated him."

Like this stockbroker, some people react to their own marriage vows as yokes, traps, prisons, or threats to their independence or autonomy, and experience them as imposed by forces other than their own will, as this man did with his own plans and decisions. They may attempt to test the "bonds" of their promises by measuring and comparing the marriage to see whether it is still good enough to stick with. In effect, they feel compelled to bring the marriage license up for renewal several times a year; it is never a done deal. People for whom a promise is a trap sometimes move in with a lover and cohabit for years, seemingly contented—until they get married. Then everything goes haywire. Sooner or later, sometimes shockingly soon, they abandon the marriage, offering some vague reason—boredom, suffocation, restlessness, loss of the old "spark," or intolerable frustration. The same thing can happen even when the couple don't marry but move in together or perhaps only "go together." Some feel trapped even though they have made no overt promise; they feel that the relation with the cohabiting lover has gradually become governed by *implicit*, unspoken promises. Then they feel compelled to dispel the trust in order to reassert freedom from the silent promises. Naturally, their partner then begs for assurances—promises—and that demand, of course, only intensifies the other's ambivalence.

Love skeptics often argue that marriage vows are impossible for mature adults in much the same way that a promise to become a cardiologist is impossible for a five-year-old. They say that no one can really know whether love will last for twenty, thirty, or more years; nor can anyone predict whether they would resist extra-marital love if love for a spouse waned (or even if it didn't). Who can ever be sure that the powerful sexual drive will not suddenly break loose from the marriage bonds? Love comes and stays or it doesn't, they say, and no magic words of promise can force it or prevent infidelity. Furthermore, our love and intentions toward the beloved rest on our present-day understanding of who that person is and on who we ourselves are. You can't seriously promise that your future unknown self will love that future stranger, so no one can really promise lifelong love and fidelity. All marital vows—so the argument goes—are at best futile and at worst fraudulent, a tradition that should die.

But there are good answers to these arguments. As for that future "stranger" we are supposed to find ourselves married to, most people who marry in their midtwenties or later will tell you, decades on, that with all the changes of age and experience, the spouse is still the same person, not a stranger at all, just as they themselves are, though changed and matured. In crucial ways, adults control who they become as they age. Control over what we will do and who we will be in the far future is a type of freedom that comes with the growth of adult capacities. In profound ways, children are shaped and controlled by their rearing and school-ing. But as adults, they develop capacities that, within the limits of social and physical realities, let them take charge of themselves and their future. The capacities that enable this freedom are those that are fundamental in promise-making, wedding, and loving (and also in planning finances, education, parenthood, and all the other prerogatives of adulthood). Being psychologically adult means realizing that you are ready to set your own life's course, shape who you will be, judge the character of the one you love, and have good grounds to believe in your shared ability to pivot when the world requires it or when you see that you erred.

We have excellent empirical evidence that young adults are actually very good at predicting their future marital affection so long as they are not *too* youthful when they marry. Most people who marry between their midtwenties and early thirties don't divorce, especially if they were raised in intact families, finished college, or have a good job. But couples don't marry on the basis of a statistical safe bet; they marry on the basis of justified trust in their feelings and themselves. They feel that they know what they can promise someone, and that they know when to trust someone else's promises.

When people love in the way that ordinary, loving husbands and wives love each other, they know more or less intuitively that love like theirs is permanent simply because it's that kind of love. They recognize that it's like *other* permanent loves in their lives. And what if they have no such loves? Then—in one of life's bitterest injustices—their choice of a life's mate is more likely to go wrong. Having loved and been loved is how we learn to love and to recognize when we love and when we are loved, and what that means. Those of us who were shorted in love have to work hard to learn how to do it.

Furthermore, these arguments against the vows don't take into account one central fact: that the very act of taking marriage vows in a ceremony has a powerful psychological effect. For people who can take vows seriously, the near prospect of actually taking vows, witnessed by all the people who matter most to them, creates a dramatic, emotion-charged public moment. It sets in motion a process of psychological reorganization, subterranean, unconscious changes that people resort to poetry to describe—becoming one flesh or half one's soul and the like. These are moving and pleasurable experiences. Of course, the same prospect helps a few people realize on the eve of the wedding that they are not ready for marriage. One clergyman describes two such cases:

> In the hours before a wedding I was telephoned repeatedly by an alternately tearful and relieved bride to say that her fiancé had called it off or had decided to go through with it. Eventually I insisted on postponement since I would not be sure when he said "I will" whether he meant it. A more dramatic example happened to a colleague. When asked "Wilt thou take this woman?" the groom fainted. Blaming summer heat and nerves, after an interval my colleague repeated the question. Again the groom fainted. Though offered money and threatened with a lawsuit, the priest refused to continue on the grounds that actions speak louder than words.
>   . . . [T]he bond of marriage has its roots at a level deeper than consciousness.

In a traditional ceremony, unless one or both of the couple are ducking the meaning of their words, the presence of witnesses, representing social conscience and social backing—the third party— makes them feel the vows as a serious undertaking, which, in turn, helps to set in motion these powerful internal processes—and the wedding actually helps to marry them emotionally as well as legally.

And, for what it's worth, our social scientists have often been curious about whether promises really do make any difference— especially promises *in public*. Their studies show that making public promises actually does result in a higher level of doing what's promised—much higher in some cases. As you can imagine, there are an enormous number of variables these studies must juggle, and the statistics depend on what is promised, who promises, and how it is promised. But studies comparing marrying with merely living together give reliable evidence that formal marriages are much less likely to break up than cohabitations. Having a public ceremony helps, and it need not be large or lavish. One justice of the peace plus a good buddy or two make it public. A wedding small enough to be intimate and affordable but just large enough to amplify the significance of the ceremony is the happy medium that nearly always works best.

People who see only dim prospects for marital happiness tend to be critical of marriage vows, especially vows of permanence and fidelity. People who take vows seriously, who both understand and *like* the idea of vows, are more likely to carry them out. A willingness to stand up before family and friends and avow love and fidelity on the part of two people who respect promises means something. It's not a guarantee, but it's an excellent sign, and its absence raises questions. From the other side of things—the side of the society witnessing the promises—social skepticism about marriage and marriage vows weighs negatively on a couple's chances, and social support is a strong plus.

Two people whose sense of self and self-control reaches into the future will find warmth and comfort in the prospect of loving each other until death parts them. For wedding vows to fulfill their purpose, the ability to take pleasure in an imagined shared future life is indispensable. Vows are an ancient and still powerful means to take control of time.

Chapter Three

THE EVOLUTION OF
THE MARRIAGE VOWS

═══════════════════════════════════

Thonked be God that is eterne on lyve,
Housbondes at chirche dore I have had five.

—Geoffrey Chaucer,
The Wife of Bath's Prologue

I f you've ever sat in a courtroom and felt the hair stand up on the back of your neck when the bailiff commands "All rise," or if you've found yourself unexpectedly weepy at a wedding, you have experienced the formidable power of a rite. A verbal rite uses familiar, fixed words to create social realities. It relies on well-known phrases to convey meanings and to create emotions that aren't just mine but ours. It creates a common ground among people here and now, as well as with past and future generations. Rites unite us in common knowledge and common feeling, making us feel less alone—and, if you're thinking that could be either good or bad, all prisoners in the dock and also the fainting bridegroom of the last chapter will agree with you. Rites exist for dark times, playful times, and happy ones like birthday parties, with cakes, candles, wishes, and singing. They're sociocultural riches everyone can help themselves to. Some call on us to toe the line when we need to; for example, when as a juror on oath we seek to be just in exercising the terrible power to deprive a fellow human being of liberty. The wedding rite, which unites the couple with each other and also with the wider social world, is a time-tested way to increase the couple's chances for success when taking the awesome step of joining with a partner for the rest of their lives.

In the Middle Ages, when most people could not read or write, spoken words cemented relations in economic, social, and political life, and also in love. Vows and oaths were taken before witnesses, using familiar phrases, verbal formulas that everyone would understand. Oral rites survive today in religious services, courtroom trials, ball games, oaths of office, and weddings.

Feudal Roots: *Vows of Homage and Fealty*

Marriage vows originated in feudalism. Just as the relationship between lord and vassal was created by solemn public vows, so was the relationship between husband and wife, and the vows that spouses made to each other resembled vows of vassalage in several ways and were probably modeled on them.

In European and Anglo-Saxon feudalism, there were two kinds of vow between lord and man: the vows of homage and of fealty, which were often but not always taken together. In a vow of homage, the vassal made himself the lord's "man." This meant that he promised loyalty, respect, obedience, and service—work or military service under the lord's command—as well as counsel when the lord needed it. The lord undertook the lifelong obligations of lordship: protection of the vassal and observance of customary limits on his power over his vassals. A pledge of homage was made kneeling, the man's hands between the lord's, to indicate submission; it was sealed—accepted—by the two kissing each other on the mouth. Thus it was said to make the vassal the lord's "man of mouth and hands." The kiss strongly suggests that feelings were considered part of this relationship. It was personal.

A vassal swore fealty by laying his hand on a holy relic and pledging his "faith," or fidelity, in formulaic words. The promise of faithfulness, which committed him to protect and serve the lord's interests and welfare, was required in order to receive a fief—a grant of land—for life. The fealty vow imposed on the lord specific reciprocal obligations of loyalty and faith to the vassal that were defined by custom—unmentioned in the words of the vow but understood by all. The vow of homage could not be broken by mutual consent; it held until one of them died or committed a substantial breach of the vow, which would release the other. The vow of fealty, however, could be broken either by mutual consent or by a unilateral breach.

Vows of homage and vassalage were honorable. They did not create serfs or "servants" or low status. (Masters and servants did not seal their relationship with a kiss and hand-holding.) Titled nobility were vassals to kings. As the medievalist F. L. Ganshof explains, the undertaking of fealty by vow or oath implied *freedom* on the part of the oath-taker. The obedience of the vassal to his lord, on account of his oath, was actually obedience to *himself*, his own will—unlike the forced obedience of a serf or slave. Although these vows centered on economic, military, and political relationships, they also created a lifelong *human* bond—and one that held "no matter what."

Historians have pointed out obvious similarities between such feudal vows and marriage vows. Both created a set of mutual rights and obligations, and until early in the twentieth century both required service and obedience from one person in exchange for protection and support by the other. In both cases, the vows created a *status* defined by established custom and law. Both kinds of vow created a complex lifelong relationship, with economic, legal, moral, emotional, and psychological dimensions. Both had to be undertaken freely and voluntarily to be valid, and, in the case of homage, were sealed by a kiss and were dissolvable by one party only if the other were unfaithful, and not by mutual consent. It was a very short step from vows of fealty and homage to marriage vows.

The very words of the marriage vows sound like feudal vows— although the modern ear hears this resemblance in reverse. To us, feudal vows sound oddly like marriage vows, which are among the few we are likely ever to hear as living words. Here is a vow of fealty from 757, reportedly taken by Duke Tassilo III of Bavaria to the Frankish king Pepin III:

> To that place [Compiègne, in northern France] Tassilo came, duke
> of the Bavarians, . . . and commended himself into vassalage by his
> hand; he swore many and innumerable oaths, setting his hand on
> the relics of the saints, and he promised faithfulness to King Pepin
> and to his sons . . . , with rightmindedness and steadfast devotion,
> in accordance with justice, as a vassal should to his lord.

"Faithfulness" here means loyalty to Pepin's welfare and interests. The phrase "as a vassal should to his lord" shows that the vow incorporates the customs and values that governed relations between lord and vassal. For many centuries afterward, the same phrase appears in the wedding "consents," in couples' promises to act as "a wife should to her husband" and "as a husband should to his wife," that is, according to well-understood custom and right.

In the tenth century, Anglo-Saxon laws give this formula for an oath of fealty:

> Thus shall a man swear fealty oaths[:] By the Lord, before whom this relic is holy, I will be to _____ faithful and true, and love all that he loves, and shun all that he shuns, according to God's law, and according to the world's principles, and never, by will nor by force, by word nor by work, do ought of what is loathful to him; on condition that he keep me as I am willing to deserve, and all that fulfil that our agreement was, when I to him submitted and chose his will.

The Old English word translated as "keep" in this vow (healdan), which later also turns up in marriage vows, means to "protect," "keep safe," or "maintain"—the lord's reciprocal obligation to the vassal. The Anglo-Saxon formula is notably more attentive to language and style than both the preceding and following examples. It uses rhythm, repetition, and punchy words to give the vow dignity and power.

Here is the efficient but comparatively flat vassals' vow of homage to Count William Clito of Flanders in 1127 CE:

First they did homage in the following manner. The Count demanded of the future vassal if he wished without reserve to become his man, and he replied "I wish it"; then, with his hands clasped and enclosed between those of the count, their alliance was sealed by a kiss. Secondly, he who had done homage engaged his faith to the prolocutor of the Count in the following words: "I promise by my faith that from this time forward I will be faithful to Count William and will maintain towards him my homage entirely against every man, in good faith and without any deception." Thirdly, all this was sworn on the relics of the saints.

Before the count will accept the man's vow, he asks for assurance that this is truly what the man wants to do—whether he gives his oath willingly and wholeheartedly, "without reserve." When the man replies "I wish it," he *consents* to the relationship; it's his firm and settled choice. But he actually becomes the count's vassal only when he says the words of the vow of homage—"I promise by my faith . . ." and so on—with assurances of truth and good faith. The same two stages, consent followed by vow, form the structure of the wedding rite.

Anglo-Saxon Sources

No record exists of wedding vows as early as the Anglo-Saxon fealty oath. Yet the people who made or heard such vows in military, economic, and political life were also busy falling in love and marrying, and there is irrefutable evidence that they also swore love. Some of this evidence appears in a pair of startling and moving poems, written in Old English, from the tenth-century *Exeter Book*. (I use Richard Hamer's translations.)

In the first, "The Wife's Lament," the wife refers to her absent husband as her "lord"—a customary way of speaking of a husband—and to her failed attempt to join and serve him. She speaks of their "vows" to let nothing part them but death, and how it is now as though their marriage and love had never existed:

> I ever suffered grief through banishment.
> For since my lord departed from these people
> Over the sea, each dawn have I had care
> Wondering where my lord may be on land.
> When I set off to join and serve my lord,
> A friendless exile in my sorry plight,
> My husband's kinsmen plotted secretly
> How they might separate us from each other . . .
>
>   . . . We had vowed
> Full many a time that nought should come between us
> But death alone, and nothing else at all.
> All that has changed, and it is now as though
> Our marriage and our love had never been.

In the second poem, "The Husband's Message," the speaker in the poem is a rune-stick on which the absent husband has carved his message to his wife, a prince's daughter. The message asks for reassurance of her love, assures her of his own "great loyalty" and "thorough love," and joyfully urges her to rejoin him. The rune-stick reminds the wife of the "vows between you both," and how her husband swore before God that as long as he lived he would keep "the bond and pledge of faith" that they "frequently" made in former times:

> He bids me tell you, then, who carved this wood,
> That you, bejewelled, should yourself recall
> In your own secret heart the vows and oaths
> That you both made in former times together.
> . . .
> About the former vows between you both,
> I understand he coupled in his oath
> Heaven and earth, and joined thereto himself
> That he would keep, as long as he has life,
> Truly with you the bond and pledge of faith
> Which you made frequently in former days.

So the couple have exchanged vows, before Heaven and earth, of *faith*; vows, that is, that pledged to be devoted to each other's interests and welfare, loyal, and true, until death, just as marriage vows do.

Scholars read this poem as referring to a marital relation, although the "frequent" pledges mentioned in the last quoted line and "full many a time" in "The Wife's Lament" sound more like lovers' vows than marriage vows. However, other sources from this period also refer to repeated vows—like Tassilo's "many and innumerable" oaths, which I quoted above—when the reality, clearly, was a single, public occasion in which this alleged flood of repetition seems quite unlikely. These references to numerous, repeated pledges in the poem, just as in the report of Tassilo's vow of fealty, seem to have been simply rhetorical, emphasizing that it was truthful and wholehearted, just as today we might say "He swore up and down."

A third Anglo-Saxon source of hints about marriage vows in the Middle Ages is an ancient legal formula, the "Be Wifmannes Beweddung." It dates from early in the eleventh century, sometime before 1023, and in Old English prescribes "how a man shall betroth a woman, and what agreement there ought to be." The word "wed" in Old English meant a pledge or promise. To betroth a woman was to become engaged to marry her in a hard-to-break form of engagement. At the end of the first millennium, long-standing custom among the propertied classes in Britain and in much of Europe made marrying a two-stage process: first, a formal betrothal, with a marriage contract and negotiations over property settlements, and second, a marriage, which might come soon or, as when young children were betrothed by their parents, years later. According to the text, this is what "it is right" for the bridegroom to do to betroth a woman:

1. If a man desire to betroth a maiden or widow, and it so be agreeable to her and her friends, then it is right that the bridegroom, according to the law of God, and according to the customs of the world; first promise, and give a "wed" [pledge] to those who are her "foresprecas [advocates]," that he desire her in such wise that he will keep her, according to God's law, as a man shall [should] his wife; and let his friends guarantee that.

2. After that, it is to be known to whom the "foster-lean" belongs: let the bridegroom again give a "wed" for this; and let his friends guarantee it.

3. Then, after that, let the bridegroom declare what he will grant her, in case she choose his will, and what he will grant her, if she live longer than he.

The third paragraph repeats the final words of the Anglo-Saxon vow of fealty, quoted above, where the vassal says that he "chose his [lord's] will." The suitor is instructed to declare what he will give his betrothed if she should "choose his will," words that unambiguously indicate a relation between man and wife like the relation of lord and vassal. This echo of the words of the fealty oath suggests that the maiden, too, might, if she accepted the man, make a promise that affirmed that she chose his will.

The "Be Wifmannes Beweddung" gives us a rich account of Anglo-Saxon betrothals but leaves us in the dark about actual weddings. Marriages were certainly celebrated, and "liturgical" books—texts of church services—show that the priest might have visited to say a prayer or bless the couple's marriage bed or house, or the wedding party may have attended church. Family and friends would gather, sometimes tucking the pair into bed together or even watching to confirm that consummation actually happened. Parties occasionally grew raucous. Among the poorer social orders, informal marriages were probably common, a simple setting up house together, perhaps under parental supervision or with a priestly visit or blessings.

An Anglo-Saxon Marriage Contract from around 1016

The Anglo-Saxon marriage contract excerpted below involved two wealthy and powerful families. It is not a contract between the maiden and her suitor, Godwine, but between her father, Brihtric, and Godwine. She is not even named. The agreement is struck "in the witness" of high-ranking churchmen and a crowd of friends and relatives. Clerics of high rank stood surety for Godwine's promises, and their presence gave weight to the agreement and certainty and publicity to its performance, but they played no specifically *clerical* role in the proceedings.

> *Here in this document is made known the agreement which Godwine made with Brihtric when he wooed his daughter; first, namely that he gave her a pound's weight of gold in return for her acceptance of his suit, and he granted her the land at Street with everything that belongs to it, and 150 acres at Burmarsh and in addition 30 oxen, 20 cows, and 10 horses and 10 slaves.*
>
> *This was agreed at Kingston in King Cnut's presence in the witness of Archbishop Lifing and of the community of Christ Church, and [other clergy, friends, and relatives].*
>
> *And when the maiden was fetched from Brightling, there acted as surety for all this Aelfgar, Sigerid's son, and Frerth, the priest of Folkestone [and other clergy and friends]; . . . Every trustworthy man in Kent and Sussex, thegn [noble] or ceorl [churl], is aware of these terms.*
>
> *And there are three of these documents; one is at Christ Church, the second at St. Augustine's, the third Brihtric has himself.*

Although records of Anglo-Saxon wedding customs are sparse, it is certain that whatever vows the marrying couple may have taken, they said them outside, not inside, the church. Despite the church's centuries of influence and keen interest in marriage and marriage law, at the end of the first millennium, it still regarded marriages and weddings as secular matters, and respected local nuptial customs. But things were about to change.

The Era of Church Dominance

In the twelfth century in the south of England and in Normandy, church manuscripts began to record wedding rites that centered on *explicit promises* about the core relations of marriage. No one knows whether or how long they may have existed before they were recorded. Some scholars have suggested that long before anyone wrote down wedding vows in service books—perhaps centuries before—couples were reciting them. The Anglo-Saxon poems in the *Exeter Book* quoted above give their view some support. Another reason to think they are right is the great similarity among English portions of the vows that appear in church manuscripts, where the Latin shows much more dissimilarity. This suggests that the translation is from English to Latin, not the reverse. Yet a third reason is the fact that for centuries wedding vows were used only in the Anglo-Norman region and not elsewhere, as one would expect if a rite was rooted in the folk custom of a specific region.

Again, we know that the wedding vows were not promulgated by the church in Rome, which has always held firmly to a policy of noninterference in local wedding styles and customs. (Only in 1969 did it introduce a rite of vows, one that contains phrases echoing the old Anglo-Norman one.) Given that the medieval church was the only reliably literate agency with an interest in domestic matters like weddings, it is no surprise that the only written records of wedding rites are church manuscripts, and that these appear only after the church took a more muscular role in marriage and related matters—as we will see below.

The custom of marriage by vow arose roughly in tandem on both sides of the English Channel—at least in extant records. Some scholars date the earliest Norman church texts a few decades before English ones, but if the vows were in use before any church manuscripts recorded them, the question of which side first used vows remains open. The many versions of the wedding rite now in use around the world bear signs of descent from the English one first recorded in 1549 and still in use today. For these reasons, this chapter glances at a few moments in the rite's English history, but with one eye on Normandy.

The Magdalen Pontifical

What seems to be the earliest English record of a marriage ceremony that contains a wedding vow is a church manuscript from the twelfth century called the Magdalen Pontifical. It's in Latin, but in practice the priest's questions to the couple, and their answers, would all have been in Middle English. The text prescribes that the ceremony take place outside, at the door of the church. The church door was the customary site for significant gatherings of many kinds—baptisms and other religious ceremonies, as well as secular matters, especially those that involved promising and swearing, such as settling legal disputes and business bargains. Words uttered at the door to the church implicitly called on divine witness even if the deity was not named. Also, because this was a public place where friends, relatives, and gawkers could observe and listen, it met the need for plenty of human witnesses—a need made explicit in a Norman wedding rite from the same period as the Magdalen: "Before everything, those who are being united in the bed of marriage come before the door of the church *in the witness of many*" (emphasis added). Live witnesses to public ceremonies served the same role that county court records serve today. They both spread the interesting news of marriages and helped prevent scofflaws from concealing or denying a marriage. It gave protection against bigamy and against seduction with false promises of marriage, and it helped to establish clear lines of parentage, inheritance, and other legal rights and obligations created by marriage.

Outline of a Medieval Wedding

Until the sixteenth century, most weddings in England that happened at the church door (and many did not) were similar to the one described in the Magdalen Pontifical. First, the priest addressed questions to the group of friends and relatives gathered there for the wedding and to the couple themselves. Were the couple cousins or otherwise too closely related by blood or affinity? Marriage even to distant cousins was forbidden except by dispensation from the church. Did either have a living spouse from a prior marriage? Bigamy and polygamy were forbidden. Had either taken a vow of celibacy? Did anyone know of any other legal impediments to the marriage? If the answers are all satisfactory, the couple then say their marrying words. The woman's "patron"—her father or other guardian (in the Magdalen rite, the patron and the priest both, though this was not typical)—gives her hand to the groom. After the vows, the dowry was given or its terms read out; the ring and coins representing the groom's gifts to the bride were blessed.

The groom had one last striking solo speech. Repeating his words after the priest, he now tells the bride: "With this ring I honor thee, with this silver I endow thee, and with my body I wed thee." Then, timing his actions to coincide with the naming of the Trinity, he recites, repeating the words after the priest, "In the name of the Father, the Son, and the Holy Ghost," and puts the ring first on his bride's thumb, then forefinger, and then her middle finger, not what we now call the ring finger. (By the fifteenth century, the ring usually went on the fourth finger, but earlier it not uncommonly went on the third.) The groom's graceful little speech evokes the full character of marriage as honorable, material, and sexual, and concludes the marrying portion of the ceremony. Many variations on this speech appear in other sources. It is also used in earlier rites that lacked vows. Little altered, it's still part of the Anglican nuptial ceremony in use today. (Modern couples may both say these words.)

After this, there are prayers and blessings by the priest, and the wedding party, singing, finally enters the church for more prayers and blessings. The couple prostrate themselves before the altar. (In some rites, the couple kneel or stand.) Then it's time for the kiss. But, to our surprise, in the Magdalen rite the groom kisses the priest first and the bride second.

The wedding vows come after the questions about the lawfulness of the marriage that are addressed to everyone gathered at the church door. Like many modern wedding rites, they have a question-and-answer format. The priest asks both bride and groom two brief questions. In the manuscript the man's questions are given in Latin, and the priest is instructed in Latin to ask the woman the same questions. The first question for both, translated somewhat stiffly, is "[Do you] want this woman/man?" Like Count William's preliminary question to his vassals as to whether they really wanted to become his man, this one aims to establish consent—whether they freely choose to marry. In colloquial English the question was probably something like "Do you want [or is it your true wish] to marry Osric here?" The prescribed Latin answer to the priest (as it was to Count William) is "Volo"—literally "I want." But in English, even Middle English, the answer would be "I do," meaning "I wish it," or "I do want to marry her/him."

The second question, again translated literally, was this: "[Do you] want to keep her/him, in God's faith and your own, in health and in sickness, as a Christian man/woman should keep his wife/ her husband?" But in English it was, in my view, likely phrased "*Will you* keep her/him . . ." The answer, again, is "Volo" in Latin, probably "I will" in English. The Latin verbs in the script, which literally translate as "want," are simply the best the scriptwriter could do to capture the tricky English use of "will" in promises and oaths—as in the fealty oath: "I will be to _____ faithful and true . . ." So used, "will" made a promise, and still does today. The English answer to the second question would have been a promissory "I will," because the words "in God's faith and your own" are a standard phrase of the time used to signify a serious promise, and all but conclusively show that the question calls for a promise in answer.

In this early script, both bride and groom promise to "keep" their mate "in sickness and health" "in the way that Christians should." This marital promise resembles the fealty oath in several ways. It, too, calls on custom. "As a Christian man/woman should his wife/her husband" echoes the words in the vow of fealty—"as a vassal should his lord." It calls on both of the couple to "keep" their spouse, just as the vassal called on his lord to keep him as he was willing to deserve to be kept. "Keep" translates the Latin word "servare," which means to keep safe or unharmed, take care of, maintain. These early marriage vows, however, are also unlike the vows of homage and vassalage in a striking way. They are *identical for man and woman*—vows, almost, of mutual marital homage. They make a dramatic statement of a kind of real equality between the couple.

The Norman Conquest of Marriage

Soon after the Conquest, in the late eleventh century, William the Conqueror issued an ordinance that separated church and lay jurisdictions in Britain. In Anglo-Saxon law, they had been one. The ordinance gave the church exclusive control over laws governing spiritual matters and classified marriage, divorce, and the legitimacy of children as spiritual. Normans quickly replaced Anglo-Saxons in the upper levels of the church hierarchy. Marriage law became church law. Norman bishops issued regulations that priests in local parishes were obliged to follow.

Some decades later, one church luminary, Peter Lombard (c. 1100–1160), bishop of Paris, worried about legal ambiguities as to whether a couple were married or simply betrothed—with good reason, given the vagueness of even church-scripted rites like the Magdalen Pontifical's. Uncertainties were even more likely in all those many marriages that happened with little or no witnessing and ceremony. No law *required* people to marry on the church steps or in the presence of witnesses, and the church recognized secret or "clandestine" marriages. In around 1150, Lombard set out a verbal formula intended to prevent disputes over whether a couple were only betrothed or were married. Words of espousal in the future tense—I *will* marry you—made, he said, a betrothal, a binding engagement, not a marriage. Words of espousal in the present tense—"I take you as my husband/wife"—made a marriage. Only unequivocal "words of the present" made marriage, and they were not only necessary but sufficient. If two people said the present-tense sentence to each other, they were married. Saying the words constituted the act of marrying.

Lombard's marrying words quickly became de rigueur. Early in the thirteenth century, the diocese of Sarum (Salisbury) issued a statute, number 84, titled "Concerning the (correct) form of contracting a marriage," which required the use of Lombard's words: "[W]e command that priests teach [both] marrying persons this form of words in French or English: I N. take you as mine."

The Roman Catholic Church calls Lombard's marrying words a "consent," as did Lombard himself. The thinking behind this is that consenting to marriage *is* marrying. But the Anglo-Norman tradition follows the Magdalen rite's feudal formula: consenting is what you do *before* you marry, as a precondition. To find out whether a couple freely consents, you question them to see whether they really want to marry and understand what marriage means.

Not everyone regards Lombard's efforts to provide a bright-line test for the existence of a marriage as successful. Here is some head-shaking commentary on the subject by the great nineteenth-century historians of English law, Sir Frederick Pollock and Frederic Maitland:

> The scheme at which [the canonists] thus arrived was certainly
> no masterpiece of human wisdom. Of all people in the world
> lovers are the least likely to distinguish precisely between the
> present and the future tenses. In the middle ages marriages,
> or what looked like marriages, were exceedingly insecure. The
> union which had existed for many years between man and
> woman might with fatal ease be proved adulterous, and there
> would be hard swearing on both sides about "I will" and "I do."

In a world where divorce was legally impossible and annulment nearly so, and the *only* way out of a bad marriage was to show that *there was no marriage*, it is asking a lot of a mere formula of a half dozen words to forestall the kinds of legal quarrels Pollock and Maitland describe. But in the Anglo-Norman region, Lombard's formula soon became part of longer recitals of a kind unusual or absent in the rest of the world. The "words of the present" got combined with a string of promises. The combination has the look of a reconciliation of Lombard's rule with an independent, perhaps secular, tradition.

The "words of the present" appear in English texts of wedding rites in the late thirteenth century. In a form for the "marriage blessings" in Latin from Westminster Abbey from around 1300, the priest asks the man whether he takes the woman as his wife and then he adds: in the faith of God *in old age*, as well as in health and sickness. This is a vow to stay with her for her whole life, a vow of permanence, added to the older vow to be steadfast in sickness and in health. A Latin rite recorded in the service book of Evesham Abbey, also around 1300, has both man and woman vow to "take" and "keep" the other "in feebleness and also in vigor"—which might be a reference both to health and to age and hence to the unlimited life of the marriage. A note appended to the Evesham rite around 1400 calls for them to take each other "from this hour on, for as long as we both live." Although the church had long forbidden divorce, these vows are among the earliest recorded ones to make permanence the explicit, sworn promise of the couple themselves.

The Sarum Rite

The most important version of the wedding rite was recorded in the Sarum "Missal," a manual or record of church practices in the diocese whose mother church is the Salisbury Cathedral, built between 1220 and 1258. ("Sarum" is the Latin name of Salisbury.) Sarum's practices, including its marriage rite, became dominant throughout Britain. Its wedding rite is the penultimate source of the words of the modern versions of the traditional wedding vows. Dozens of Sarum manuscripts survive, some in parts and some entire, dating back to the thirteenth century and forward to printed versions from the early sixteenth century.

To start with the bad news about Sarum: from the beginning of its history to the end, every version of its wedding rite had unequal vows for men and women. This was not true throughout Britain. The Magdalen Pontifical, the Evesham Abbey rite, and a Hereford rite all show identical vows for men and women. In one way or another, Sarum's unhappy differences between men's and women's vows persisted down to modern times.

Sarum weddings had the same overall structure called for in the Magdalen Pontifical: a gathering at the door of the church, preliminary questions as to the lawfulness of the union, the dowry, ring, consent, vows, groom's speech, kiss, and more. But, unlike the Magdalen Pontifical, Sarum rites from around 1300 had only one all-purpose question, with no preliminary consent, and included the "words of the present" that the church regarded as consent. One manuscript presents a question only for the man. Conceivably, a priest might have been expected to understand that the woman was to say the same words. But this seems doubtful in light of another Sarum text from around the same time that includes questions for both man and woman. The question for the man has "words of the present" and also inserts the word "lawful": "Do you, in God's faith and your own, take this woman as your lawful wife, to keep, as a Christian man should his wife, in sickness and in health?" The woman's question omits both the "words of the present" and also the important words that clearly signify a solemn vow—"in God's faith and your own." In fact, her question calls for no vow at all and no "words of the present." It only asks for her consent: "Do you want to have this man as your lawful husband to keep faith with him in all things?"

The groom's vow shows how churchmen handled the literary challenge of combining Lombard's formula with what were (as I tend to think) traditional promises, like those in the Magdalen Pontifical—"to keep," "as a Christian should," "in sickness or in health," as well as others. The solution was to append the promises to the marrying "words of the present." Lombard's words create a marital relationship, and the promises appended to them commit the groom to a specific kind of marriage—not just any kind but one that he would persevere in under hard circumstances like illness—in fulfillment of what their religion asked of him in marriage. The woman, however, only consents and makes no vows like his. But this imbalance was not universal in the Anglo-Norman world, and it is righted in Sarum a century later.

In a rite from around 1400, Sarum has adopted the two-part

format, which I have been calling consents and vows (a common but not universal usage). The consents are a series of promises that reply to the priest's questions. The vows, like the groom's in the 1300 rite above, combine Lombard's marrying words with promises. Only the latter promises are formal vows, shown by the phrase "and thereto I plight thee my troth," and the couple address these to each other. (The promises of the consents and formal vow may all be called "wedding vows" today.) The manuscript still gives the consents in Latin (translated below), but the vows are now in Middle English. The bride's consent includes a promise to "obey and serve" the groom. His consent is the same as hers but for those words, which are in italics below.

> [Bride's consent question] Will you have this man as your hus-
> band *and obey and serve* him and love, honor, and care for him in
> sickness and in health as a wife should her husband? (emphasis
> added)

After they each consent, both take vows, but not in the question-answer format. Rather, they repeat the words after the priest, as in the modern ceremony, and address their words to each other, not, as in earlier rites, only to the priest. This text calls for the couple to promise to keep each other as husbands and wives should, not as *Christian* husbands and wives. The woman's vow has all the words given to the man, but, alas, also a few more. The vows for the first time appear in the manuscript in Middle English and these, too, show a lengthening list of promises appended to the "I take you" "words of the present."

[Repeating after the priest]

[Groom's vow] "Ich *N.* take thee *N.* to my wedded wif for betur
for wors, for richere for porere, in sekenes and in hele, til deth
us departe, as holy churche us ordeineth, and ther to y pligte
the [thee] my treuthe: . . .

[Repeating after the priest]

[Bride's vow] "Ich *N.* vndurfonge [take or take possession]
the [thee] *N.* to my weddud housbonde for betere for wors, for
richere for porere, in sekenesse and in helthe, *to be boxom to the*
[thee], as holy churche us ordeyneth, til deth us departe, and
ther to y pligt the [thee] my treuthe: . . ." (emphasis added)

(Some versions, earlier and later, have the woman promise to be
"bonere and buxsum." Both words are explained below.)

These vows show other novelties, whether newly invented or old
tradition newly recorded by English priests. Mostly, the new material
is absent in French rites. The triplet "for better for worse, for richer
for poorer, in sickness and in health" begins to show up here and
there in England in the late fourteenth century, but French rites of
the same period have, at most, "in sickness and in health," not the
classic English three. The words "til dethe us departe" are new,
though "in old age" had been used earlier. And the woman also
vows "to be boxom to the[e]," more words that the man does not
reciprocate. Man and woman both say, at the end of their vows, "and
thereto [that is, to those promises] I plight my treuthe." "Treuthe,"

or "troth," as the judge who officiated at my first wedding accurately explained, means good faith and truth. In that time and place, these were powerful words that indicated a solemn vow.

The groom's final solo speech is somewhat different from the Magdalen version. It lists four gifts, not three:

> [Groom's solo speech] "With this ring y the wedde, and this
> gold and sulvere y the geve, and with my body y the worschipe,
> and with my worldliche catel [goods, chattel] iche the sese
> [seise, give possession]."

The new fourth gift is all his worldly goods. Also, now he weds her with the ring and *worships* her with his body—unlike in the Magdalen Pontifical, where he *weds* her with his body. In Middle English, "to worshipe" meant "to honor," so the change to "with my body I thee worship" is both pretty and rather sexy. This version made it into the English Book of Common Prayer and is still there.

And what isn't here that later appears? Jumping forward a century, the printing press has been invented, and a Sarum manual appears in type. It continues to give the consent promises in Latin, and the vows only in English. The early sixteenth-century consents more fully address the couple's readiness and willingness to marry, now calling for a clear promise of *sexual fidelity* for both man and woman. Both will "forsake all others" and "keep only" to the spouse. The church will not look past men's extramarital sex; he is to have no lovers, plural wives, concubines, or anyone else. (Women's sexual infidelity was never looked past.) He alone promises to "hold" her, somewhat gratuitously, seeing as how both of them are about to vow to "have and hold." It looks almost as though the groom's "hold" was added only to balance out the bride's "obey and serve"—about which more in a moment.

Here is a translation of the couple's consents in a Sarum manual printed in 1506. The text instructs the priest that the consent questions are to be asked "in the hearing of the audience" at the church door in the mother tongue.

Sarum (1506) Consents

[Bride] *N.*, Will you have this man as your husband, to obey
and serve him; and love, honor, and keep him in health and
sickness, as a wife should a husband, and, forsaking all others
for him, keep only unto him, so long as you both shall live? The
woman answers: I will [Volo].

[Groom] *N.*, Will you have this woman as your wife, to love,
honor, hold and keep her, in health and in sickness, as a husband
should a wife, and forsaking all others for her, keep only unto her,
so long as you both shall live? The man answers: I will [Volo].

The vows open with Lombard's present-tense "I take you"—conjoined with solemn promises of the fundamental, core elements of the marital bond. A brief note to the priest explains that these are "words of the present"—words, that is, effective to create marriage. The words "to have and to hold" had been added sometime in the fifteenth century. The woman's vows still include the words "to be bonere and buxum in bedde and atte bord."

Sarum (1506) Vows

[Groom] I, *N.*, take the, *N.*, to my wedded wif, to haue and to holde fro this day forwarde, for better for wors, for richer for pourer, in sykenesse and in hele; tyll dethe vs departe, if holy churche it woll ordeyne, and therto y plight the my trouthe.

[Bride] I, *N.*, take the, *N.*, to my wedded housbonde, to haue and to holde fro this day forwarde, for bettere for wors, for richer for pourer, in sykenesse and in hele, to be bonere and buxum in bedde and atte borde, tyll dethe vs departe, if holy churche it woll ordeyne, and therto I plight the my trouthe.

The consents and the vows, between them, by this time include all the core elements of the marital bond: love, care and protection, respect, fidelity, permanence, steadfastness. The consents alone pledge to love, honor, and keep; none of these three promises—not even love—are included in the vows, though "hold" can mean what "keep" does. With one exception, the vows address only the strength and unconditional nature of the marriage bond. The exception is those vexing vows by the woman to be "bonere and buxum." But it's important to understand that those words, at that time, did not mean "pretty and plump," as "bonny" and "buxom" do today. "Bonere" or "bonaire," according to the *Oxford English Dictionary*, meant at the time "well-bred, gentle, courteous, kind, complaisant"; "buxum" or "buxom" meant compliant, amiable, obliging, submissive, or meek. "Borde" was a table used for meals. So the woman promises to be kind and courteous and obliging in bed—sexually, in other words—and at meals. She must promise to be a pleasing and pleasant mate, but presumably he is entitled to be as grumpy at dinner and disobliging in bed as he wants. This is insulting and unfair, and, happily, the final version of the vows, which appears a few decades later, gets rid of it.

As for the wifely service and obedience promised in the consents (not yet in the vows), though they are new in the Sarum rite, they were old in Christian doctrine. They are not good, but perhaps not quite as bad as they seem on first reading. They continue to give the marriage vows a bad name today even though many versions dropped them more than a century ago, and secular, Roman Catholic, and most Protestant versions have long since dispensed with them. Whyever they came to be included, they should be read as the feudal vows that they were. They strongly resemble vows of fealty and homage, especially the Anglo-Saxon vow of fealty presented earlier, which included an explicit promise of submission to the lord's will. Service and obedience are precisely what a vassal promised a lord, and loyalty and protection were what a lord promised his man. In swearing service and obedience, the bride promises to a man only what dukes and knights, in vowing fealty, also promised to a man—or what men who sign up for military careers implicitly promise superior officers. Her vows clearly *subordinate* her but do not *demean* her or her sex.

Though modern thought may consider subordination inherently demeaning, feudal thought saw no dishonor in such a vow. In fact, if service and obedience are vowed, not commanded or forced, they are performed as a matter of self-government and free choice. That she is asked to vow acknowledges her as an independent, self-controlling moral agent; hence it also respects her. It is a discouragingly narrow and ambiguous slice of freedom, but it's nonetheless true that women's ancient service and obedience acquire a different meaning when they are undertaken by vow. This new vow was, to that extent, actually a small but significant step in the right direction. It meant that women assumed these duties as their free choice, as self-imposed law. They were not sold, compelled by their parents, abducted, or forced into concubinage by circumstance or tyranny. The man's and woman's vows are otherwise mutual, and, we must not forget, in all other respects—permanence, love, honor, sexual fidelity, loyalty—husband and wife are moral equals in ways that expand a woman's rights and status beyond those of her ancestors. This is far from today's idea of full equality, but it's progress. That she receives promises of love, honor, fidelity, permanence, and loyalty are advances; all mark a warmer, more humane understanding of marital relations.

Yet despite all that can truly be said in defense of the Sarum rite, it is hard not to look admiringly and wistfully across the channel to Normandy. Remarkably, no Norman marriage rites between 1100 and 1543 that I have seen included any words in women's consents or vows comparable to "bonere" or "buxum" and none included "obey and serve."

The next major change in the marriage vows was to come soon, four decades later, and it is the subject of the next chapter.

Chapter Four

HOW THOMAS CRANMER
BROUGHT LOVE TO MARRIAGE

Now that marriage has ceased to enjoy the safeguards of a system of social compulsion, the only possible basis on which it can rest is individual choice . . .

Once we ask ourselves what is involved in choosing a man or a woman for the rest of one's life, we see that to choose is to wager . . .

The attempt to minimize or to conceal the fact that, when considered objectively, a choice of this kind is a wager fosters the belief that everything depends on wisdom or on a set of rules, when actually everything depends on a decision . . . [although] to the extent that probabilities can be weighed, it would be stupid not to weigh them . . .

To choose [a mate] is to say . . . "I want to live with you just as you are."
For this really means: "It is you I choose to share my life with me, and that is the only evidence there can be that I love you."

—Denis de Rougemont, *Love in the Western World* (1940)

In 1556, aged sixty-six, Thomas Cranmer, archbishop of Canterbury, was burned at the stake for heresy and treason. Before this cruel death, he had spent two and a half years imprisoned, isolated from family and friends, threatened, browbeaten, beseeched, and abused. Weakening, he repeatedly recanted his earlier religious convictions. Under canon law, this should have saved his life, but his recantations were rejected as insufficient, and Queen Mary insisted that he die. On the day of his execution, in a passionate and unexpected public speech, he recanted his recantations. They had betrayed his true faith, he declaimed, and he promised to punish the hand that signed them. Chained to the stake, he plunged his right hand into the fires that were about to consume him and held it there, repeating that it was "unworthy" and "hath offended."

Cranmer shows up on-screen and in plays and novels, most recently in Hilary Mantel's *Wolf Hall* trilogy about Thomas Cromwell, as well as in biographies and innumerable histories. His story is full of vengeance, hatred, courage, ambition, politics, and faith. To an extraordinary degree, it's also about marrying, weddings, and love.

Cranmer's Rebellious Love

Cranmer's life was full of nuptial joys, tangles, and catastrophes, not all of them his own. A youthful marriage ended with the death in childbirth of both his wife and their baby. He became a priest, earned respect, and made a modest ascent through the church hierarchy. When Henry VIII sought to have his marriage to Catherine of Aragon annulled, in defiance of Catholic doctrine that forbade divorce or, except in narrow circumstances, annulment, Cranmer's views on how and whether annulment might get papal approval made a favorable impression on the king and his advisors. He became a chief player in the drama that ended with Catherine set aside and Henry married to Anne Boleyn—events that launched Cranmer into a career of great political influence.

Before this, Cranmer had been sent to Europe to make contact with Protestant thinkers in hopes that their ideas would provide scriptural justification for the annulment. In 1532, carrying out this marital mission in Nuremberg, he himself fell in love and married again, this time to the niece of a Protestant theologian. Of course, as a Catholic priest, he was forbidden to marry. But, at the time, many Lutheran clergymen in Nuremberg had rebelled against that restriction and married, and their example influenced him. He was well aware that his marriage would get him in trouble in England. Worrisome as this was, it soon became alarming in unforeseen ways when, as a newlywed lingering in Nuremberg with his bride, he received a letter from the king appointing him archbishop of Canterbury—a remarkable and unexpected elevation. He returned to England but apparently kept secret from the king and everyone outside his intimate circle the existence of a wife and, later, children. When clerical marriage was made legal in 1549 and he let the existence of his family be known, the facts took his enemies by surprise.

Throughout his career, Cranmer finagled and pushed for clerical marriage, but Henry thought priests should remain celibate. Meanwhile, Cranmer careened from one dangerous political crisis to another as he gained or lost favor with the king or the king's counselors. In 1539, the Act of Six Articles made him so fear for his own and his family's safety that he rushed them out of England.

More dangers were created by Henry's continuing marital night-mares, as he went through wife after wife, annulling the marriages with Catherine and Anne of Cleves, beheading Anne Boleyn and Catherine Howard, losing Jane Seymour to death in childbirth, and, upon his own death, leaving Katherine Parr a childless widow. Cranmer survived all these crises, but Cromwell, Henry's chief minister, was not equally lucky.

After initially forwarding the king's marriage to Anne of Cleves, a German who spoke no English, Cranmer finally opposed it vigorously and sincerely on the grounds that such a marriage would not make the king happy. But for weighty polit-ical reasons Cromwell pushed for it. Cranmer's and Cromwell's biographer, Diarmaid MacCulloch, gives this account of their dispute over the proposed marriage:

> [Archbishop Cranmer] was solicitous for Henry's personal
> happiness, as a royal chaplain should be. He said he did not
> wish to see the King "marry without [outside] the realm." The
> Archbishop *thought it most expedient the King to marry where that he*
> *had his fantasy and love*, for that would be most comfort for his
> Grace." Cromwell snapped back furiously, "There was none
> meet for [his Grace] within this realm." One can see exactly
> [the political motives] why the Lord Privy Seal [Cromwell]
> should say that . . . Cranmer retorted with spirit "that it would
> be very strange to be married with her that he could not
> talk withal" . . . In the event the supposedly politically naïve
> Cranmer got the King's psychology right; if only Cromwell had
> listened to him. (emphasis added)

In his concern for the king to marry someone who answered to his fantasy—liking or desire—and love, Cranmer showed more sympathy for him than did Cromwell, and also more wisdom, as the marriage to Anne turned out to be anything but "expedient." Henry agreed to the marriage despite his misgivings, having never met his future bride, and Cranmer's fears quickly proved accurate. Henry married her in early January 1540 and immediately rejected her. The marriage was annulled on July 9, 1540, and Cromwell's bad advice led to his fall from favor. He was beheaded a few weeks later, on July 28, 1540. On that very day, July 28, Henry privately married Katherine Howard.

Cranmer escaped Henry's deadly wrath, but in the longer run his own role in Henry's marital dramas was equally fatal. His early support for deposing Catherine of Aragon made him his most dangerous and lifelong enemy—Catherine's daughter, Mary, whose unappeasable hatred eventually brought about his death.

The 1549 Book of Common Prayer

The Book of Common Prayer is the all-English-language book of church services that Cranmer was called on to create following Henry's breach with Rome. He completed this work, the first official book of Anglican services, in 1549. For its wedding rite, Cranmer used most of the Sarum rite. The ceremony that he wrote survives essentially intact (spelling aside) in the 1662 Book of Common Prayer still in use in the Anglican Church. Cranmer is thus the man who comes closest to being if not the father, then at least the uncle or godfather of the traditional wedding vows. We can point to specific paragraphs and words in the wedding rite that he was responsible for, which are few but powerful. They are the only words in the rite to which we can assign an author—and a famous one at that. The rest comes down to us through the anonymizing mists of history. Cranmer was a master of prose and persuasion, and the Book of Common Prayer is universally regarded as an English masterpiece.

The opening words of the Sarum wedding rite were spoken outside, at the door of the church, in accordance with ancient tradition. It began, "We are gathered here, brothers . . . ," and proceeded into questions to those assembled about the lawfulness of the marriage. (See Appendix I.) As a whole, it was stiff, legalistic, and cool. But Cranmer's 1549 version calls for "*the persones to be married [to] come into the bodie of the churche, with theyr frendes and neighbours . . .* ," and the priest's first words to the wedding party, spoken inside the church, greet "*deerely beloved frendes,*" not "brothers." Cranmer's rite begins with a welcoming, brisk, sweet homily on the meaning of marriage, which portrays it in warm tones and comes to the question of lawfulness only at its end. His preface, consents, and vows, along with those in the Sarum manual, are printed in full in Appendixes I–III (at the end of this book). His changes to the groom's solo speech that begins "With this ring I thee wed" (see Appendix III) are entirely, and successfully, stylistic.

Marriage, the priest begins, is "an honorable estate" instituted by God "in paradise, in the time of mannes innocencie." We finite humans did not create marriage. God did, at the beginning of everything. Adam and Eve were already married in the Garden, *before* they ate the forbidden fruit and were cast out, and marriage is something innocent and good that we carried out with us. Neither a consequence of our fallen nature nor a punishment for it nor forced on us as the lesser of evils, it furthered happiness even in paradise, where Adam was lonely until Eve was created. Cast out into a world where we confront suffering, evil, danger, and death, we still have marriage, and it's still innocent, good, and desirable.

The priest reminds the wedding party that the first miracle Jesus performed was at a wedding: the miracle of turning water into wine, when the hosts' stores ran out. Jesus's associating himself with marriage in this friendly way "adorned and beutified" the institution.

Just How Much Wine?

In case you haven't looked into the question, Jesus turned six pots of water into wine. Each pot held two or three firkins, and a firkin was ten to eleven gallons—so somewhere between 120 and perhaps close to 200 gallons of wine, on top of what they'd already drunk. (It was one big wedding.) And, so the tale goes, it was very good wine, too, better than the stuff they'd already drunk and run out of. It's a story that gives a thumbs-up to celebrating weddings with good things to eat and drink.

But, as good sermons do, this one follows the good news with more sober thoughts. Marriage serves serious purposes and is therefore an honorable and respected estate, not to be taken "lightelye, or wantonly, to satisfie mens carnal lustes and appetites, like brute beastes that have no understanding: but reverentely, discretely, advisedly, soberly, and in the feare of God. Duely consideryng the causes for the whiche matrimonie was ordeined." Those causes were standard church doctrine: for procreation of children, for avoidance of fornication (extramarital sex), and for companionship, this last elaborated in Cranmer's words as "for the mutuall societie, helpe and coumforte, that the one oughte to have of thother, both in prosperitie and adversitie." "Coumforte" doesn't only mean to console or condole, as does our modern word "comfort." At the time, "strengthening" and "encouragement" were also among its central meanings. Consolation and condolence—comforting—are appropriate only in "adversitie," not in "prosperitie," but we would appropriately "coumforte" our team to clinch an impending victory. The French root was "fort," meaning "strength"; "con," which becomes "com" in English, was a grammatical intensive, that is, a prefix that gave force or emphasis. An illustrative sentence from 1464 (with mostly modernized spelling): "If . . . they make any gathering in coumfort of Richard, sometime king, they to be punished as traitors." Samuel 2:2 in the Coverdale Bible (1535) says, "Let youre hande now therfore be comforted, and be ye strong." The phrase about giving "aid and comfort" to enemies was already ancient when it showed up in 1788 in the new US Constitution as part of the definition of treason.

Cranmer's introduction to the rite shows his commitment to the ideas of the Reformation. It presents marriage as innocent, honorable, pleasurable, beneficial, and serious in purpose—something intrinsically good. It is consistent with many aspects of sixteenth-century Catholic doctrine, but not with its ideal of celibacy or its generally cooler attitude toward marriage. The Council of Trent (1563), convened by Rome to counter the Protestant Reformation, had this to say on the subject: "If anyone says that the married state excels the state of virginity or celibacy, and that it is better and happier to be united in matrimony than to remain in virginity or celibacy, let him be anathema."

In accordance with tradition, Cranmer's 1549 rite was divided into two separate tranches, the consents and the vows. Both the consents and the vows deleted the old "as a husband/wife should a wife/husband" and substituted "to live together after Goddes ordeinaunce in the holy estate of matrimony," underscoring the Protestant point that the "ordeinaunces" governing marriage are God's, not, as in earlier rites, the church's. Cranmer makes a welcome stylistic change in the couple's consents, splitting the Sarum rite's long, single question into three (see Appendix III).

The man's consent has one new promise. Now he's asked, and the woman isn't, to "coumforte" his spouse. His "coumforte" replaces "hold" in the Sarum groom's consent, perhaps to balance the wife's "obey and serve," but perhaps, also, to reflect some harsh life lessons. Cranmer began work on the Book of Common Prayer in 1547, the year of Henry VIII's death. Behind him, stretching across all his years as archbishop during Henry's reign, lay a series of sad, frustrating, potentially catastrophic, and occasionally lethal marriage issues. Given that their illicit marriage must have caused Mrs. Cranmer much fear and suffering throughout those years, it's easy to see why Cranmer might have thought it was important to mention strengthening and encouraging a worried, wearied wife in men's consent to marriage.

Cranmer's most important changes, however, come in the vows. The first six words of these were already centuries old: "I take you as my husband/wife." Cranmer deletes Sarum's "to be bonere and buxum in bedde and atte borde." For men, he adds "to love and to cherishe"; for women, he adds "to love, cherishe, and obey." The Sarum rite had a promise of love in both consents, and "serve and obey" in the bride's consent, but there was no *vow* of love for either. Before the 1549 Book of Common Prayer, love was not a vow of marriage but only a promise in the consent.

In the fourteenth through sixteenth centuries, only the consents, not the vows, in both the York and the Sarum service manuals asked the couple in English to promise that they would "love" each other, and in both, the English word "love" translated the Latin word "diligere" in the priest's script. "Diligere" has no exact English equivalent. It doesn't mean what "love" means in speeches like "I love you, darling. Will you marry me?" It means something more like "I love our state's senators and hope to meet them some day." Although the consents in Sarum's and York's manuals use the English "love" (appealingly spelled "luf" in York's), where the Latin uses "diligere," "diligere" more accurately means the esteem and respect you might feel toward a friend of the family or a respected colleague. Cicero wrote in a letter to a friend: "Why should I commend to you a person whom you yourself esteem? However, to let you know that I have *not only esteem* [diligi] *but affection* [amari] for him, I am writing to you about this matter" (emphasis added).

None of the many English rites and only one of nineteen French ones that I consulted mention "amare" or "amor." But in ancient Latin, as in modern Spanish, "te amo" is what you say to your sweetheart or spouse. (That lone French exception gives no scripts for consents or vows, but instructs the priest to inquire whether there is *amor* between the pair in his preliminary questions.) "Amo" is the better Latin term for the tender love of marriage and romance, and the clergy of that time, who certainly knew what "amo" meant, chose not to use it in the wedding rite. Still, English-speaking couples promised English "love" in their consents. They may or may not have had "amor" in mind, since the English word "love" certainly covers both loving your senator and loving your sweetheart and other kinds of love, too.

The "love" in Cranmer's vows comes in the phrase "to love and to cherishe"—an entirely new vow in the marrying words, and one that makes clear the kind of love he has in mind. Cranmer's "cherishe" meant what our "cherish" does—to hold dear and treat with tenderness—but not only that. In 1514, you might also unsaddle and then cherish your horse, meaning pet or stroke it. The word was also used for the tender, nurturing, fondling care given to children, and also the nurturing care given to plants, one's own hair, or, ironically, in Shakespeare's *Henry VI, Part 3*, to human "weeds" (by not getting tough enough with them). Cranmer's love is a cherishing love—a nurturing, adoring, fondling, tender kind of love. Cranmer's revision of the vows made marriage the natural home, and in fact the refuge, of such love in a world that too often makes little room for it.

By making love a vow, Cranmer made it *essential, of the essence*, in marriage, what it *is* at its core. This meant that marriage was, logically, available only to people who could honestly vow that they loved each other. Although the change was revolutionary, it was not perceived that way. The English word "love" had been used for more than a century in the consent promises, and wouldn't have sounded novel in the vows. Few people, even few theologians, would stop to wonder about the meaning of "diligere" versus "amare," or the difference between a promise of English "love" in the consents instead of a promise of love in the vows. The new word "cherish" slipped in with "love," under its wing, as though it were simply elaborating instead of "coumforting" an underground revolution. But "cherish" made it clear that marital love wasn't "diligere." It was "amare," the love of tender feelings, with their implicit tie to sexuality and their joy in the other person, which was to be sworn to. That kind of love can't be forced or created for economic or political purposes or to serve ambitions for status or power.

The addition of tender love to the marrying sentence made all the promises of the consents subject to the solemn vows of the marrying sentence. To vow to love someone in this way is to vow to honor and keep them, and to forsake all others. These things are part of what love means.

Cranmer's respect for love made marriage *free*—and modern, even though his preface insisted that it was as old as creation. He wrote in an age in which arranged marriages, forced marriages— and marriages exactly like Henry's with Anne of Cleves, made to consolidate political, military, or economic goals—were common in all classes. Cranmer's addition of "love and cherish" to the vows didn't change that. But it delicately taught other values and shifted the balance of power between marrying couples and those with power over them. It's harder to pressure and threaten into marriage someone whose idea of marriage includes loving and cherishing.

The vow of love meant that an unloving marriage required a false vow—and risked divine punishment. For people who took vows and divine punishment seriously, this gave lovers' hearts a theoretically decisive power over the choice of a marriage partner. Of course, arms were still twisted and children were still forced into marrying mates they did not love or hardly knew or perhaps despised. But the marriage vows, taken in conjunction with the church's growing willingness to countenance marriages without parental consent, had made them more free. Marriage for love also made men and women not equal, but less unequal. It let a woman's choice matter more. It also made a kernel of equality basic to marriage. No one feels marital love for a person they don't recognize as their equal in some fundamental way.

In the long run Cranmer's small changes meant that marriage became a quiet reservoir of freedom and equality, encouraging individualism and free choice. A right to self-determination in marriage was one that might easily spread to political, religious, and social contexts. Not that those ideas did not spring from many more obvious sources, but Cranmer's wedding rite brought them to a vast population via a text that readily engaged trust and respect—the Book of Common Prayer, which was itself a rebellion against religious authority.

The 1662 Book of Common Prayer

Cranmer's 1549 rite is practically unchanged in the 1662 revisions to the Book of Common Prayer, which, in whole or in part, is still used today in millions of marriages. "Derely beloved frendes" is shortened to "Dearly beloved" and a word or two has gone missing or been added in the priest's preface. The vows themselves are word for word what they were 1549.

Excerpts from the Anglican Ceremony in the Book of Common Prayer 1662

The Form of Solemnization of Matrimony

If no impediment be alleged, then shall the Curate say unto the Man,

N. Wilt thou have this woman to thy wedded wife, to live together after God's ordinance in the holy estate of Matrimony? Wilt thou love her, comfort her, honour, and keep her in sickness and in health; and, forsaking all other, keep thee only unto her, so long as ye both shall live?

The Man shall answer, I will.

Then shall the Priest say unto the Woman,

N. Wilt thou have this man to thy wedded husband, to live together after God's ordinance in the holy estate of Matrimony? Wilt thou obey him, and serve him, love, honour, and keep him in sickness and in health; and, forsaking all other, keep thee only unto him, so long as ye both shall live?

The Woman shall answer, I will.

Then shall the Minister say, Who giveth this woman to be married to this man?

Then shall they give their troth to each other in this manner . . .

I *N.* take thee *N.* to my wedded wife, to have and to hold from this day forward, for better for worse, for richer for poorer, in sickness and in health, to love and to cherish, till death us do part, according to Gods [*sic*] holy ordinance; and thereto I plight thee my troth.

Then shall they loose their hands; and the Woman, with her right hand taking the Man by his right hand, shall likewise say after the Minister,

I *N.* take thee *N.* to my wedded husband, to have and to hold from this day forward, for better for worse, for richer for poorer, in sickness and in health, to love, cherish, and to obey, till death us do part, according to Gods [*sic*] holy ordinance; and thereto I give thee my troth.

And the Priest, taking the Ring, shall deliver it unto the Man, to put it upon the fourth finger of the womans [sic] *left hand. And the Man holding the Ring there, and taught by the Priest, shall say,* With this ring I thee wed, with my body I thee worship, and with all my worldly goods I thee endow . . .

Just as the ceremony recorded in the Book of Common Prayer became fixed in its current forms, and couples for the first time took their vows inside the church, the powerful Protestant movement called for a radical resecularization of marriage. Civil marriage again became the rule throughout the West. In many countries, including the United States, the United Kingdom, and Italy, clerics may still serve as officiants at legally binding weddings, but civil registration or licensing is also required. In others, however, like France, only civil authorities may officiate at weddings, and religious ceremonies, though common, are without legal effect.

The traditional "American" ceremony, the secular one used in civil marriages by mayors, judges, and justices of the peace—like the one in the second epigraph to this book—removes all religious references. Otherwise it is Cranmer's sixteenth-century revision of the ancient Anglo-Norman rite, which evolved in the eleventh through the sixteenth centuries, the core of whose vows is nearly a thousand years old, and whose roots are older. The wife's vow of obedience was long ago dropped from mainstream ceremonies, religious or secular, in the United States. The American Episcopalian Book of Common Prayer deleted it in 1928. As long ago as 1789, the prudish Americans entirely deleted the husband's "With my body I thee worship"—in the words of one commentator "out of delicacy." The modern changes are, otherwise, mostly good, as is the preservation of all the parts of the ceremony that are timeless. It comes to us as an inheritance that has survived a millennium of changes and ties us to values that are fundamentally and universally human, and that cross all the historical boundaries of space and time.

II

Six Wedding Vows

Chapter Five

A BRIEF BIOGRAPHY OF LOVE

"Of course I still love him. How can you unlove?"

—Jerry Hall, about Mick Jagger,
Sunday Times, September 5, 2010

D o I still love my first husband? Of course. How can you unlove? But it was always a weak, undernourished, ambivalent sort of love, and once it got stored away in a back corner of my mind, it grew even weaker and thoroughly disconnected from my life, to the point that now I'm surprised when I stumble over it while searching through memories. It is valuable, however, as a reminder of things that I came to understand about love as a result of that painful first experience of it—things that no one thinks about as long as things go right.

The short explanation for why my first marriage went wrong is that he didn't love me. The particular way in which he failed to love was so confusing to us both that the marriage dragged on for years, with repeated separations and increasingly tense, hopeless reunions. The relationship puzzled our families and friends, too. A little professional guidance gave me the key to figuring out both why the marriage was never going to work and some general truths about love.

Four years into that marriage, I received an unexpected love letter from a man I knew, liked, and respected, someone older but under forty. On the one hand, I was shocked because I was married, which he well knew; he and I had never had an intimate conversation of any sort; and I didn't love or desire him. On the other hand, I was starved for a kind word, and couldn't help feeling pleased to get several especially nice ones from a man like him. But I dismissed his feelings as a crush and did not respond. A year or two went by, and one day he arrived at my door, uninvited and unannounced. My feelings hadn't changed, but neither had his. This time, I understood that he was not issuing an invitation to an affair but declaring the kind of love that goes beyond attraction and offers care, kindness, and concern. It was clear that my welfare, what happened to me, mattered to him, and he seemed preternaturally aware of the fact that my life was unhappy.

I never saw that man again, but his visit was a turning point for me, because his concern made me recognize vivid oddities in the marriage that I had felt but not understood. My husband responded to any troubles of mine from a friendly, well-meaning distance, rather like a kindly neighbor with whom I occasionally discussed geraniums at the mailbox. He regretted my problems, but they did not affect his own well-being or peace of mind. This extended even to serious health issues, with which he was sympathetic but somehow uninvolved. Over the years, he had breached his wedding vows more than once, and he had begun saying that he didn't want to have children until he was in his forties, which, of course, was likely to rule them out for me, as we were the same age.

It took a professional counselor to put a name to the problems. On hearing my story, her first words were, "He thinks you're his twin." He was, in fact, an identical twin, and he and his brother had the storied talents of twins—reading each other's minds, calling their parents within minutes of each other, free-associating to the same unlikely words, and so on. He needed emotional distance from me in order to preserve his deeper tie to his twin and also to preserve his fundamentally precarious sense of independent, autonomous identity. Closeness and intimacy, marital care, permanence, fidelity—these aspects of marriage made him feel merged into his mate, not an independent self. At the same time, he couldn't be happy without a twin, and I was a substitute twin who was safer than his brother, whom I increasingly thought of as my own Madame Merle, from Henry James's *The Portrait of a Lady*—someone who invisibly manipulated my life, who was informed of all the secrets of my marriage and was more intimate with my husband than I was myself. My husband always felt his best perched on the edge, neither in nor out of the marriage or twinship and able to call on whichever suited his current needs. Eventually I learned that emotional issues with separation and personal boundaries in love relations are not uncommon challenges for twins. He himself, however, was impatient with psychological explanations and instead became a critic of the institution of marriage.

I had married someone who felt his personal autonomy specifically threatened by the parts of love that called for caring and protecting each other, for fidelity and permanence—the *moral* part of love at its core. That part of love he gave to his twin. This was too far beyond my understanding to let me help him or to let him help me. We were no help to each other.

Love as the Natural, Resilient, and Enduring Basis for Marriage

In marriage, the sexual and moral parts of love are intertwined. But much current thinking doubts this. Skepticism about the staying power of love is often seen as rational caution or plain common sense. Friendship, with or without love, is often considered the best foundation for marriage. You can easily see this slippage in trust for love in the poignant self-written wedding vows posted online at wedding sites. More often than not, they entirely omit the vow of love, retreating to a pre-Cranmer style. One version suggested this compromise with the traditional words: "I *want* to love you through good fortune and adversity, while we both shall live" (emphasis added), which is not a vow but a hope, a hedged bet. Another site's "Contemporary Wedding Vows" section offered eleven sets of sample vows, only three of them with a vow of love. Five omitted it entirely. Two fudged it with ambiguous promises, and one undid it by going over the top with a vow to give "*perfect* love and *perfect* trust" (emphasis added), which sounds as though the writer considers vows merely aspirational or, perhaps, adorable absurdities, like a child's promise of the impossible. But when Cranmer added "love" and "cherish" to the vows, he had in mind something real and attainable. He probably thought that he himself had it, and certainly he thought that Henry VIII could, and should, have it, too.

Love resists formulaic explanations, and book-length ones often turn into mush by the second or third chapter. But the remaining pages of this chapter can, I hope, serve as a brief reminder of some reliable truths about love. One is the fact that almost everybody wants unending love, which means that they want marriage, even if they don't understand that they do. Ben Jonson's *Hymenaei* (1606) has this line: "Marriage love's object is." You would search long and hard to find someone who hopes that love won't last too long or that the person they love will move on to someone new, or already has someone else on the side. I can come up with only two possible examples of people who don't want love to last, neither of which fits this description exactly. The real-life one is my first husband. The fictional one is Goethe's Faust, who, in his bargaining with Mephistopheles, seeks variety and change, not satisfaction:

> FAUST. Poor devil! What can you offer to me?
> A mind like yours, how can it comprehend
> A human spirit's high activity?
> But have you food that leaves one still unsatisfied,
> Quicksilver-gold that breaks up in
> One's very hands? Can you provide
> A game that I can never win,
> Procure a girl whose roving eye
> Invites the next man even as I lie
> In her embrace? A meteoric fame
> That fades as quickly as it came?
> Show me the fruit that rots before it's plucked
> And trees that change their foliage every day!

Another truth about love is that the number of marriages that end in divorce says very little about the staying power of love. Yet the divorce rate is cited over and over as a reason not to marry. There are many people like my first husband and me, who have abnormal and unusual psychologies and make a hash of marriage. It would be odd to see our confusions as evidence of the fragility of love, rather than as evidence of our peculiar emotional problems. There are also quite a few bad people in the world, people who kill marital love with cruelty and other misbehavior. Does that reflect poorly on love? Some people get married when they are seventeen or eighteen, and within a year or two or three one or both have changed so much that their love is mostly a memory. Large and increasing numbers marry without love. After all, if love is weak and fickle, why not base marriage on good solid friendship and shared goals—kids, house, operating a business? There is no study in which people are asked whether they did this, but my private guess is that the divorce rate among those who do is far higher than for those who marry for love, and that their children may also be more vulnerable to divorce, having grown up without a model of an intimate love relationship between two people whom they admire and love passionately.

The sensible conclusion isn't that divorce is the result of love being too unreliable to base your life on. Love is highly reliable, and an excellent thing to base your life on. It strengthens relationships and increases life's good things. But some people don't find it, some people can't manage it, and love is sometimes defeated. Even so, it's also the strongest and best support any marriage can have, and once you find love, there are highly effective ways to protect it.

The love marriages of people with psyches in a broad psychologically competent range, an average share of human decency, with
some education or religion and a job, who wait until at least their
midtwenties to marry, are unlikely to end in divorce.

How to Minimize Risk of Divorce.

The figures below, published by the National Marriage Project
at the University of Virginia in 2012, describe "percentage-
point decreases in the risk of divorce or separation during the
first ten years of marriage, according to various personal and
social factors." They will show some people that their risk is
lower than they had thought. Others will see how they might
improve their odds.

	Percent Decrease
Annual income over $50,000 (vs. under $25,000)	-30
Having a baby seven months or more after marriage (vs. before)	-24
Marrying over 25 years of age (vs. under 18)	-24
Family of origin intact (vs. divorced parents)	-14
Religious affiliation (vs. none)	-14
College (vs. high school dropout)	-25

The odds greatly favor a pair of college graduates over age twenty-five with a good income, who aren't pregnant when they get married. Some of the things in this list aren't in our own control. We don't get to choose our parents, and we don't control the advantages and disadvantages they confer on us. But everyone can aim to marry at a mature age, wait for marriage to get pregnant, try to get some education, and find a job that pays a living wage, and those are the factors that count the most.

The tragedies in which love is defeated are much less common than divorces. Marriages can break up under the stress of the death or disability of a child, infertility, poverty, or career failures. Some people may push a mate away out of love for them, hoping they'll find a better life. When times are very hard or dangerous, some haven't enough courage to stand by a mate. Amazingly often, painful situations like these *don't* end in breakups, and the couple come through for each other.

The Tangled Roots of Love and Sex

The striking truth about love is not how fickle it is but how extraordinarily tough it is. The yearning for *lasting* love is the effect of powerful biological forces: the natural love of babies for their parents, parents' love for their progeny, fear of death, and love of life. Love is nature's means of ensuring that we do what it takes to reproduce; to protect and care for each other, our children, and our friends and neighbors; and to survive.

Mate Choice and Moral Merit

One study of mate choice finds that moral merit is sexually attractive. One of Mother Nature's ways of ensuring that you choose a mate favorable to survival, it suggests, is to push you to pick a *good* person, an admirable *character*, for your mate, just as she favors some beauty (and, perhaps, strong deltoids and an ability to run fast). It's a theory with detractors. One of them was a married clinical psychologist, a neighbor and friend who used to go jogging with me and another single friend, both of us just divorced. One day, puffing along in Riverside Park, we asked him how to pick a good husband. We thought *he* was a very good husband and father, proven by his wife's calm and friendly acceptance of his habit of regularly jogging with a pair of young divorcées.

"You have to pick a man like me," he said, confirming our private opinions. "A mensch." A mensch is an upright, strong, honorable man, a man of high character.

He continued, "The trouble with us mensches is, we're boring."

If this was true, the study was wrong, and women would prefer exciting men to men of high character. But it wasn't true. Our psychologist friend was a forty-something man with a bushy mustache, a paunch, a loving wife, two sweet daughters, and a tame, orderly domestic life. We didn't find him *at all* boring. Mensches of any gender are interesting and attractive to people looking for love, and, as in our friend's case, one of their menschy traits may be modesty.

The love-and-marriage skeptic tends to think of sex and love as separate things that get forced together at cultural gunpoint and in pervasive myths about love. But nature itself conjoins them; separating them would have defeated its purpose—to encourage propagation. The corollary to this is that all forms of love that aren't closely tied to sexual life—to our biology—are less permanent, less exclusive, less committal, less protective, and less tender than those that are. Relationships with friends, colleagues, teachers, and professional helpers have some qualities of love. Friendships can have remarkable depth, warmth, and loyalty, and without friends life would be cold, lonely, and dull. By and large, however, family relationships and romantic relationships, which are all built on or around (or replace or seek) biological connections, have more of the qualities on that list. Friends are *like* brothers and sisters. A beloved mate is—as millions find themselves saying and thinking—*like* a father, mother, brother, sister, all at once. Psychologists say that our relations with mates are significantly shaped by past relations with our parents—and this can be functional, if we're lucky, or dysfunctional. It's in being loved that we learn how to love, and those who grow up without ordinary parental affection, from parents or surrogates, face hard struggles in their search for love.

Psychoanalysts have steadfastly refused to back away from the theory that the adult longing for tender, exclusive, and enduring *sexual* love is rooted in the jealous love of tiny children for their parents, which, they add, braving over a century of scoffing and distaste, even has an erotic quality—a prereproductive, infantile erotism experienced in cuddling and suckling. What love is more tender, steadfast, jealous, and permanent than a child's for a parent? Brave soldiers wounded on the battlefield cry out for mother. Seventy-year-olds weep hopelessly when their ninety-something parents desert them in death. We internalize our parents to such a degree that they are a permanent part of who we are. We still love them at the ends of our own lives (and if we had troubled relations with them, that trouble may also still be with us at the ends of our lives). It's a fact that explains both how love can be permanent and how you can know when yours is. It becomes permanent when someone becomes part of you in this same way. You know the love is permanent because you recognize it. You know the depth of these feelings and what they mean because you've been there before. It's something familiar.

Love for parents creates emotional patterns that are followed later in love for a mate. The same idea is expressed in Ephesians 5:31 (with the Bible's usual male perspective): "For this cause shall a man leave his father and mother, and shall be joined unto his wife, and they two shall be one flesh." Repurposed, updated, and sexually liberated, that first love lends its tenderness, utter steadfastness, exclusiveness, and permanence—all the *moral* dimensions of marital love—to the adult sexual love between husbands and wives. We replace our parents with our mates—which is not just right, but all too right. One of the most common marital dilemmas is one partner's disappointment in a mate for not being more like an adored, idolized parent whom the other can't give up wishing for.

Preschoolers are still having a baby romance with mother or father, and they are still very physical in all their affections. They sit on grown-ups' laps, hold hands, and walk with their arms around friends' shoulders. But, magically and inevitably, usually sometime before they start elementary school, their romance with mother or father ends. A three-year-old plans to marry Mommy or Daddy, but seven-year-olds know better, and a few may already begin to develop crushes on children and adults outside the family. In primary school–age children, sexuality in most respects, though not all, largely continues in abeyance. They will be curious about sex and giggle and make jokes about it; they might play at having boyfriends and girlfriends; and sometimes they even fall in love. But full-blown sexual feelings fail to appear until adolescence, with the physical changes of puberty. From then on, in the teen years and forever after, various kinds of snuggling—originally a form of innocent infantile physical affection—serve as a lead-in to sexual excitement.

Childhood, Love, and Weddings

The powerful love for a parent lately seems more and more frequently to drive people to approach marriage as though they are clinging to childhood instead of reaching for adulthood. Some years ago (October 4, 2013), a *BBC News* Magazine article asked, "Why Is a Children's Book about Rabbits Being Read at Weddings?" The article described a wedding at which *Guess How Much I Love You*, by Sam McBratney, was read aloud in its entirety. Amazon says that this book is appropriate for children ages one through three. It's about two hares outdoing each other in poetic descriptions of their love for the other: "'I love you all the way down the lane as far as the river,' cried Little Nut-brown Hare. 'I love you across the river and over the hills,' said Big Nutbrown Hare."

According to the article, other wedding favorites are *Winnie-the-Pooh*, *The Velveteen Rabbit*, *The Little Prince*, Dr. Seuss's *Oh, the Places You'll Go!*, and *The Secret Garden*. The trend it described continues today. It dovetails with others, such as the recitation of self-composed wedding vows about childish wishes ("I promise to make your favorite chocolate-chip pancakes on Saturdays") and the appearance of teddy bears on wedding cakes and elsewhere in the ceremony.

The tie between the psychologies of adult and childhood love may explain this fashion. Perhaps the more worried people are about adult love and their marriage's chances of success, the more they retreat into a realm where love was reliable. The BBC article pointed out that as childhood texts become more popular, the verses of 1 Corinthians 13:11–13 ("When I was a child, I spake as a child, I felt as a child, I thought as a child . . .), once favored at weddings because they mark the occasion as an accession to adult love and adulthood, are heard less often.

The Birth and Long Life of Marital Love

After first falling in love, people can't get enough of their new lover and want to spend all their time together. For a while, they might become their best selves in relation to the lover. Sooner or later, they'll get used to having each other and are no longer stunned by having achieved what they feel—quite rightly—as a life- and soul-changing connection. The novelty dies fast; falling in love quickly evolves in one of two ways. Either they fall out of love (or one of them does), or the love sinks roots into both of them. If both of them fall in love, and the signs of compatibility are compelling, falling in love gradually turns into love.

Most people love only a few times in their lives. Many experience it only once, and some never do. In the nineteenth century and well into the twentieth, people expected falling in love to lead straight to marriage. Today, there is more skepticism about this experience. It's all too possible to fall for someone who would not be a good marriage partner, and one experience of failed love is not soon forgotten. After more than one, people begin to guard their feelings. The next time, they want to be sure before they make themselves vulnerable to the grave and life-altering pain of losing love.

The most important reason why people tend to have few experiences of being in love, however, is a happy one: once they are in love, they don't want anyone else. They are satisfied, and they stay that way. This is not to say that no one in love can be unfaithful; it is to say that if a person in love is unfaithful or lonely or unhappy, there is a complicated backstory to the situation. For example, it seems possible, though fortunately uncommon, for a person to be in love with two people at once. Ordinarily, this is not a doubling of pleasure but a painful, unenviable experience to which certain kinds of divided souls are especially vulnerable. It is more commonly experienced in youth, before a person has had a chance to get all of their beliefs and emotions on the same page. Mature adults grow more like one person and less like several people all fighting to live in the same body.

But our devious and controlling ur-mother, Nature, seems to have spared no efforts to ensure we choose a compatible mate. At the outset, she gives us a gentle push by endowing us with a tendency to choose people who look somewhat like ourselves. (If you don't believe this, study the photographs in engagement announcements.) Then, seeing our capacity to fall for people with whom we have too little in common to make a good match, nature gave commonality a big push. She made the experience of being in love *transformative*. If you are in love, you are a changed person, partly because *you are experiencing a kind of love that creates identifications and internalizations*. Lovers absorb each other and become more alike. They often adopt each other's expressions, ways of laughing, vocabulary, style, and tastes. Studies that document the experience use dry, dull language to describe it. Love "expands the contents of the self" or allows us to "include the other in the self" and increases "self-efficacy and self-esteem." The researchers also point out that this kind of love gives people a chance to try out new or suppressed or ideal aspects of their identity. Of course, these changes don't guarantee compatibility, but they give it a nice boost.

The intimacy between a couple who have gone through this process trumps the intimacy that either of them shares with anyone else. They identify with each other on a level that makes them capable of experiencing significant parts of their lives as belonging to "us." Husbands and wives also construct a shared set of values, a common conscience with ideals and standards that they both acknowledge, usually without ever talking about it. If their mutual influence is harmful, one or the other may be brought to do something that he or she once thought was wrong and fail to perceive it as wrong. Maybe one of them is convinced to accept cheating on their income tax. Maybe one gives up an idealistic career with a moderate salary for a fashionable, well-paid job because the other respects those things more. (That's a plot in George Eliot's *Middlemarch*; Lydgate, the deeper character, is brought down to living at the level of his shallow wife, Rosamond, because in crucial ways he is weak and blind.) The choice of a marriage partner can help someone become everything they can be or trap them in the cage of a spouse's small-mindedness.

The core of marriage is this creation of a shared psyche and a new two-person, erotically charged society. It is based on a deep and broad identification with the spouse that arises and operates at a level beneath conscious awareness. Simultaneously, the couple share an identity but also remain separate persons. If the individuals disappear or are merged wholly into, or are overdependent on, the other, this destroys the marriage. Marriage requires two separate, autonomous people capable of functioning both as independent individuals and as a couple. Not everyone finds this easy or natural or desirable, and marriage is not for everyone. Not all good, sane, attractive, lovable, admirable people are cut out for marriage, though most are, and not everyone who is cut out for marriage will want to get married or find someone to make a marriage with, but most do.

The couple's shared psyche, the effect of their shared love, stabilizes the marriage because, in times of conflict, it ensures that each partner is on both sides, his or her own and the spouse's. The part of them that identifies with the spouse also sympathizes, knows their feelings empathically, understands their thinking; it also provides enormous trust, built-in motives either to acquiesce in the other's wishes or to seek compromise, and the kind of knowledge that lets them figure out effective compromises.

In loving marriages, the partners identify with each other in the same way they identified with their family of origin—something that is natural for most people but that for my first husband was fraught and dangerous. "Identify" isn't an adequate term for what happens in ordinary marriages, because there are many kinds and levels of identification. The kind that matters here is mostly or nearly unconscious. Our parents are *ours*, and we belong to them— not in an owning way but in an identifying way that goes very deep. The psychologist and philosopher William James describes it in his chapter about "the Self" in *The Principles of Psychology* (1890) with a wonderful discussion of the "Material Me": "[O]ur immediate family is a part of ourselves. Our father and mother, our wife and babes, are bone of our bone and flesh of our flesh. When they die, a part of our very selves is gone. If they do anything wrong, it is our shame. If they are insulted, our anger flashes forth as readily as if we stood in their place; if they behave admirably, I am proud; and if they do wrong, I'm ashamed—and the same is true in the other direction." Love of the kind that James describes gives us one of life's rare escapes from ego; it's the embrace of the other person as "mine and me" that lets us care about that person in this ultimate way. This is why, if you despise yourself, you find it hard to love someone else, and also why genuine love relations are always equal relations—because you have made them into part of you. The kind of love that makes for marriage has that kind of "us" at its root.

The irony of Cranmer's free marriage built on love is that this kind of love can't be summoned at will and can't be dismissed at will. It arrives and creates its own welcome, both by what it gives and what it gets back. Like love for parents, it can be killed, but only with great difficulty and terrible pain. Unless it is forcibly uprooted by bitter betrayals, cruelty, desertion, or similar causes, it dies only when you do. This kind of love doesn't guarantee that a marriage will be lasting and happy, and many people marry without it, but it gets you, say, 85 percent of the way there. Everything favors its survival. If you want a lasting, happy marriage, your best bet is to find somebody to love.

Chapter Six

A MUTUAL ADMIRATION SOCIETY

"In vain have I struggled. It will not do. My feelings will not be repressed. You must allow me to tell you how ardently I love and admire you."

—Darcy to Elizabeth, in Jane Austen
Pride and Prejudice (1813)

Honor is as indispensable to love in the twenty-first century as it was when Jane Austen wrote about Mr. Darcy falling in love with Elizabeth Bennet. In his first, failed declaration of love for her, he stupidly tells her that his pride is so offended by the thought of having her absurd family as in-laws that he has been resisting his own love. He makes clear that his love includes high honor for Elizabeth herself, despite the fact that she can't offer him money, great beauty, or simple respectability, let alone advantageous family connections—the worldly things that he felt entitled to as a very rich, handsome man from a respected family. He loves Elizabeth for herself, a moral achievement given the downsides of the relationship, but it isn't enough. He has to grow as a person, become a better man, to be worthy of her before she can honor him in return, and thus fall in love with him.

Anyone who is in love finds something worthy of respect, something excellent, in the one they love. This doesn't mean they're always right about it; it's possible to be deceived in someone's character and also to be misled about what human qualities are worth respect. Some people admire power, and love people capable of gaining it. There are those who admire fraudsters and cold-blooded hit men and regard them as more courageous and smarter than other people.

You can be attracted to someone you don't honor, but you can't be in love with them. Honoring each other is an essential dimension of love. Once you start honoring someone, you may also find yourself compelled to love, unable not to love them. Darcy could not help himself. He so honored Elizabeth that against his will he loved her. Being loved is also *felt* as an honor, and for that reason can be humbling. It can make you think: Am I worth this? A truism of pop psychology is that people without self-respect tend to devalue those who love and honor them.

The institution of marriage is addressed primarily, centrally, to us humans as sexual beings. It would be strange to vow lifelong sexual fidelity to someone you didn't desire sexually. It's certainly possible to honor someone and not love them, but respect and admiration are closely linked with sexual attraction. Plain, penniless little Jane Eyre (in Charlotte Brontë's 1847 novel) turns down a marriage proposal from St. John Rivers, a handsome Anglican priest whom she admires. He wants to marry her because he thinks she is tough and humble enough to be a hardworking missionary's wife in India. He doesn't love her and has no romantic or sexual interest in her. Jane rejects him and chooses Rochester, whom she loves for himself, even though he did wrong. He, in return, had always made it clear that his feeling for her included delight in her oddness and sexuality, and that his love was adoring. He honors her for her strength, intelligence, quaintness, independence, and integrity. Jane chooses him over the more respectable, nobly motivated, and handsome St. John Rivers even though Rochester is newly impoverished, nearly blind, scarred, and sinful. She likes to sit on Rochester's knee, but it's hard to imagine St. John Rivers with anyone on his knee.

Her choice is, on its surface, a choice of sex appeal over a religious duty of self-sacrifice, but it's not only that. Clearly, Charlotte Brontë, and her surrogate, Jane Eyre, don't believe that St. John Rivers is the superior character. He is cold. He is ready to sacrifice a young woman's life to virtuous ministry in a place where her health and happiness will be at risk from infection, heat, overwork, and more. He does not honor Jane and, undervaluing her, does not love and protect her. Jane courageously holds out for her right to be loved, rather than used, and her right to love. She forgives Rochester and honors him for his own courage, his capacity for love and kindness, and more.

A List of Gifts

In the traditional rite, the promise to honor is in the consents, not the vows. The rite contains a second reference to honor that makes the connection between honor and sex explicit. That the connection is true and valid will be recognized by anyone who ever fell for an otherwise unlikely lover. The line occurs in many surviving texts of the rite, including the Book of Common Prayer, the Sarum rite, and some among the very oldest—the Magdalen Pontifical and the Bury St. Edmunds missal from between 1125 and 1135 CE, almost a thousand years ago. It comes just after the vows, and it's a speech that only the groom made back then. The groom recites as he puts the ring on the bride's finger: "With this ring I thee wed, *with my body I thee worship* and with all my worldly goods I thee endow . . ." (emphasis added). To "worship," centuries ago, meant to "honor," and it was used in reference to human agents and human acts as well as to the deity and divine acts. In the words of the rite, honor and sex are not only *not* separate and inherently in conflict; you actually do the former with the latter. Modern readers may well wonder just how that works.

The words don't mean that *all* sex is honoring with one's body, but that between us two who love each other it is. The pretty words "with my body I thee worship" are part of a list of gifts. Gifts are a traditional way of paying homage, or of honoring someone. Around the world, people honor their gods, heads of state, friends, family, and adored performers and artists with gifts on holidays, birthdays, funerals, and other important days—wedding days. The groom's list of gifts includes the wedding ring, all his worldly goods—and also his body. Honoring her with his body means that he gives her his body and his bodily desire for her in the exclusive sexual relationship he has just avowed, with its implicit promises of love, pleasure, and the hope of children. (Of course, this is mutual, and today we want words that say so.) His sexual devotion and gift of his body are an expression of esteem and a natural part of love. If you have had the good fortune to experience desire for someone you love, you know that's how it is (or you will if you reflect on it for a moment). The desire you experience for someone who is the most important person in your life, the one you will partner with in creating a family, making a home, pursuing work. When you love someone that way, love transforms the sexual experience with its tenderness. This doesn't happen in less important relationships. Certainly FWBs, casual sex, and bought sex can bring sexual gratification and excitement, but not this kind.

The sexual "worship" in the rite is a rather intimate matter to announce to a crowd of wedding guests. (As chapter 4 noted, in 1789 Americans deleted the blush-inducing words "with my body I thee worship.") But the version in the 1662 Book of Common Prayer is still in use in the Anglican Church around the world. It continues to remind the world that all love, by its very nature, honors; marital love honors a whole human being—a physical, sexual, spiritual, and moral being.

Honor and the Perception of Someone You Love as Separate

The kind of honor that the rite mentions twice does *not* mean respect for a person's worldly successes or standing. It's not about Nobel Prizes, medals, wealth, degrees, power, beauty, talent, or fame. Love intrinsically and naturally honors the beloved as the beloved, not for these second-rung good things, and despite their human imperfections. Not that we don't value and take pleasure in their accomplishments, their wonderful cooking, their dimples, the way they walk, or the fact that legislators turn to them to find out whether bridges are safe for people to drive over. On the contrary, we love those things about our sweethearts, just as we accept their failures and annoying and infuriating aspects—because we love them.

Love often fails early in a relationship because the lovers collapse into each other. You can't honor someone without some psychic distancing from them, without stepping back and seeing what they are apart from yourself and your relationship. You can't love someone who isn't "other" to you. Honor, in good relationships, is always there, but not always conscious. There are moments when you feel your separateness and rediscover this element of respect in your feelings. You see what the other person is, *objectively*, and how much they mean to you. Honor is about the things in your beloved that *made* you love them. Naturally, there are many songs about this. ("You made me love you. / I didn't want to do it.")

The vow of honor doesn't call on you to idealize and overestimate the one you love, or to believe they're superior to others in some way. It calls on you to honor them for who they are, humanly speaking. It's such a hard thing to put into words that, usually, the essential role that honor plays in marriage gets acknowledged in indirect ways. Songs and poems say it better than analysis, and Shakespeare's Sonnet 130 says it best of all:

> My mistress' eyes are nothing like the sun;
> Coral is far more red than her lips' red;
> If snow be white, why then her breasts are dun;
> If hairs be wires, black wires grow on her head.

I have seen roses damasked, red and white,
But no such roses see I in her cheeks;
And in some perfumes is there more delight
Than in the breath that from my mistress reeks.
I love to hear her speak, yet well I know
That music hath a far more pleasing sound;
I grant I never saw a goddess go;
My mistress when she walks treads on the ground.
   And yet, by heaven, I think my love as rare
   As any she belied with false compare.

"Rare" here does not mean "uncommon." Shakespeare uses it in another sense that, according to the *Oxford English Dictionary*, was familiar in the sixteenth and seventeenth centuries: "unusually good, fine or worthy; of uncommon excellence or merit." The poem is saying that he finds excellence and value in her that does not rest on the qualities idealized in this series of metaphors, with their literal falsehoods. Because he loves her, he honors her for the unique person she is, for herself. What she is in herself belies not simply any particular comparisons but shows how, in love, all comparing is false.

Chapter Seven

ON OUR OWN:
LOVE AND LAW

Man Punches Great White Shark to Save Wife: "You Just React." *The woman was bitten on her right leg and taken to the hospital.*

—ABC News, August 16, 2020

Pregnant Woman Rescues Husband from Shark Attack in Florida. *A pregnant woman dived into the sea in the Florida Keys to save her husband from an attacking shark . . .*

—BBC News, September 24, 2020

Husband Steers into Crash to Save Wife, Unborn Child. *He swerved to take brunt of collision with car that was coming at them head-on.*

—*Today*, September 13, 2010

Man in Malaysia Rescued from Tiger by Wife Armed with Ladle. *Han Besau used kitchen utensil to club tiger, which had pounced on husband while he was hunting squirrels.*

—*The Guardian*, February 14, 2011

*Man Gave Own Life to Save Wife from Joplin Tornado. NBC's
Brian Williams talks to 25-year-old Bethany Lansaw of Joplin, Mo.,
who lost her husband Don during the deadly tornado. Don saved his wife's
life by covering her with his own body as they took shelter in their bathtub.*

—NBC News, May 24, 2011

The vow to "keep" seems to be one of the first two wedding vows to appear in a historical record. The mid-twelfth-century Magdalen Pontifical (described in chapter 3) includes a wedding rite that instructs the priest to ask both man and woman: "Will you keep [her/him], in God's faith and your own, in sickness and in health, as a Christian [man/woman] should keep [his/her wife/husband]?" Each was to answer: "I will." The primary meaning of "keep" here is physical. It's about looking out for your mate's health and safety. It means to protect, guard, support, take care of, or keep safe—not "retain." That's also part of what the very ancient phrase "to have and to hold" means in the "I take you" sentence found in later versions of the rite. Our modern word "hold" descends from the Old English "healde" (healdan), which meant, among other things, to "keep," in the sense of "guard," "preserve," "defend," "maintain," or "support."

Sometimes, the vow "to keep" enjoins serious hardship and sacrifice—a fact that inspires admiration for the marriage bond when circumstances put it to dramatic test, as in the news headlines in this chapter's epigraphs. Most people in the modern Western world are never called on to save the one they love from sharks, tigers, or tornados. We hope we will rise to the occasion if and when we are, but in ordinary circumstances, the vow "to keep" is about ordinary types of protection and support—meals, housing, clothes, medical care, and whatever else is needed for physical safety and survival. When your mate is too sick to get up, you bring them medicine and meals in bed. You remind them to set the house alarm system or watch out for the ice on the road or make a doctor's appointment; perhaps you beg them to give up skydiving after their back operation. You cut back on spending so that your spouse can quit a job that injures their mental or physical health. Or you keep working at a job you despise, to keep the roof over your heads and food on the table.

When Does the Law Step In?

The vow to keep your husband or wife is unique in yet another way. What this vow promises is also, broadly speaking, enforced by law, and, at least on paper, it's law that still has some teeth. Until well into the twentieth century, this was also true of other marriage vows. The law stood behind the vow to stay together for life and the vow to forsake all others. The law never punished failures to love and cherish, except through the narrow back door of allowing divorce or separation in cases of cruelty and abuse. (Presumably the law never figured out how to prove, disprove, or remedy mushier failures to love or cherish.)

Modern law is dramatically different. It permits divorce at will, even against your mate's wishes, even if you have children together.

Even the minority of states with criminal sanctions for adultery still on their books (sixteen at last count) stopped enforcing them half a century ago. Every state still forbids bigamy, but that may not mean much. The state of Utah was admitted to the union only on condition that it forever prohibit polygamy, and its state constitution contains that prohibition. Yet, polygamy flourishes in Utah, and in 2020 the state decriminalized it and made it an "infraction," like a traffic violation, committed by taking out more than one marriage license. Nothing, so far, stops a man (it's always a man) from setting up house with three or four or forty or more "informal" or "religious" wives, so long as he takes out only one marriage license.

One way in which the law, like the vow, requires us to "keep" our spouses is through the legal duty of married people to provide necessary medical care for each other and to render each other aid in emergencies. Except for public safety professionals like doctors, firefighters, and EMTs, people aren't obligated to offer others such aid unless the person needing help is their spouse or child or someone else they have a relationship with, or other special circumstances exist. If you fail to aid your spouse, you risk lawsuits or even criminal charges, including homicide if your spouse dies as a result.

A second legal doctrine, one that sounds exactly like a duty to keep your spouse, is the duty of support. Ancient in the law, it still exists but is now gender-neutral—about which more below. Until well into the twentieth century, it meant that husbands were required to support their wives and that wives were required to render domestic services to their husbands, but the reverse was not true. Supporting the wife meant providing her with the necessities of life, or "necessaries": food, clothing, shelter, and medical care. If the wife bought such "necessaries," the husband was liable to pay for them even if she incurred the debt without his knowledge or permission. This requirement simply enforced his legal duty to support her—and this was fair, when you consider how rigidly the law in earlier times restricted women's ability to earn their own living.

In practice the duty to support wasn't overly generous to wives. Courts had to juggle support obligations with the legal need to protect "marital privacy." A man could be stingy, lazy, or irresponsible without violating his legal duty to provide necessaries. A Nebraska case from 1953 is still assigned to law students to teach them how marital privacy limits the necessaries doctrine. The plaintiff in *McGuire v. McGuire* was a woman who had been married for thirty-three years to a man with "a reputation for more than ordinary frugality." The case is notable for the remarkable honesty of both Mr. and Mrs. McGuire. Mr. McGuire agreed with the not-very-flattering facts about him alleged by Mrs. McGuire. It is also notable because this was not a divorce case. Mrs. McGuire wasn't suing for alimony, and the couple lived together even as they fought it out in court. The dispute was solely about what the husband's legal obligations were.

The dreary facts were these: Many years earlier Mrs. McGuire had inherited a share in a chicken farm, which she worked and which for a long period gave her income. She used the income to buy the household's groceries, miscellaneous household necessities, and her own clothes, and to pay for infrequent trips to visit her daughters. When Mrs. McGuire, at the age of sixty-six, could no longer work her chicken farm, Mr. McGuire began for the first time to pay for their groceries. Mr. McGuire, who was seventy-nine years old at the time of trial, never bought her any clothing, except for one coat three or four years before the trial. He had paid for several abdominal operations for his wife, however, and they lived on his farm. Mr. McGuire was, in fact, a prosperous and successful farmer, with a substantial yearly income plus what were in those days very substantial assets, including over a hundred thousand dollars in government bonds. That would be the equivalent of more than a million dollars today.

Mrs. McGuire wanted the court to order Mr. McGuire to provide for her more adequately. She wanted him to modernize their kitchen, which lacked a sink with running water and other modern facilities. She wanted him to put in a new furnace and get a car with a heater. Their unheated car was more than twenty years old, Nebraska had bitter winters, and they were elderly. She wanted him to pay for one trip per year to visit her daughters (his step-daughters). He refused to do any of those things. Mr. McGuire, in short, was something of a miser, and he refused to provide his wife with what would have been quite a low standard of living even in the early 1950s, especially for people with their income and assets.

The lower court ruled in favor of Mrs. McGuire and ordered Mr. McGuire to put in appliances and furniture, get a new car with a heater, pay for one trip a year for her to see her daughters, and more. But when Mr. McGuire appealed, the Nebraska Supreme Court overturned all of those orders, pointing out with acid understatement that "the husband's attitude toward his wife, according to his wealth and circumstances, leaves little to be said in his behalf." "Necessary expenses" meant something minimal as long as they lived together as a married couple. Had Mrs. McGuire moved out, the court implies, it would have been able to order Mr. McGuire to support her in a manner more suitable to his wealth and status. But, as matters stood,

> The living standards of a family are a matter of concern to the household and not for the court to determine . . . As long as the home is maintained and the parties are living as husband and wife it may be said that the husband is legally supporting his wife and the purpose of the marriage relation is being carried out. Public policy requires such a holding.

One obvious way to make the law kinder would be simply to broaden or replace the idea of "necessaries." A 1979 Supreme Court decision resulted in a wave of new state legislation that did just that. *Orr v. Orr* struck down an Alabama law on alimony because it imposed spousal support obligations exclusively on husbands. The court held that the Alabama law violated the equal protection clause of the Fourteenth Amendment.

To comply with *Orr*, some states jettisoned the doctrine of necessaries altogether. More commonly, they retained it but applied it equally to husband and wife, as in this Texas statute:

(a) Each spouse has the duty to support the other spouse.

(b) A spouse who fails to discharge the duty of support is liable to any person who provides necessaries to the spouse to whom support is owed.

Other states, like California, wrote gender-neutral laws that, unlike Texas's, omitted any reference to "necessaries." California's law has been interpreted to mean that the couple must support each other in a manner befitting their means and way of life. In California today, Mrs. McGuire might win her lawsuit, and perhaps the spouse of a tech billionaire could hold out for a forty-room mansion or a trip to Paris for new high-fashion clothes once or twice a year. Some modern statutes substitute "marital purposes" or "family expenses" for "necessaries," creating an indefinitely expandable set of obligations. Illinois courts have held that family expenses may include funeral expenses, carpets, household help, or even jewelry (depending on what the jewelry is for). But here's the rub. Although these laws do take away limits on what "necessaries" are, some of them also entitle creditors to go after both spouses or either of them no matter which one made the purchase or what each spouse's financial situation may be. If this sounds to you as though the law in some states might serve to help creditors more than beleaguered spouses, you are not the first to have that thought.

Heart Balm

Decades ago, laws backed up marriage vows in yet another way: through a set of statutes called "heart balm" laws. These laws survive in only a few states, but well into the twentieth century, many state laws offered "balm" for wounds of the heart that affected matrimony, permitting injured parties to bring lawsuits for damages; some carried criminal penalties. Heart balm laws aimed

particularly at protecting women from, for example, the heart-
less but not uncommon evil of "seduction"—inducing a woman
to engage in sex with lying promises of love and marriage—a
seriously blackguardly way to behave in an age before easy birth
control, when the only "career" open to most women was marriage and family, and loss of virginity or unmarried motherhood
might easily render a woman permanently unmarriageable. Heart
balm actions also included civil suits for alienation of affection and
"criminal conversation," or "crim con," as it was called (against
the person who seduced or had an affair with your mate), and
breach of promise to marry.

The point of these laws was to remedy some real harms and
wrongs and to discourage out-of-wedlock births, infidelity, abandonment, and divorce. It's not crazy to think that to some extent
these laws did in fact accomplish those goals. It's also not crazy
to think that the law became needlessly cruel when it abolished
heart balm suits, which aimed at preventing and mitigating some
of the most personally destructive injuries that can be experienced,
or to think that those laws might even have helped prevent some
domestic and intimate-partner violence. Not crazy perhaps, but
also short of justifying a return to the old heart balm suits, which
eventually became a legal disgrace in their own right.

As women gained rights, and social values changed, it became
clear that these laws also served as open invitations to blackmail by
unscrupulous gold diggers. In an earlier era, women had been seen
mostly as victims of bad men, but in the first decades of the twentieth
century the public began to class women among the malefactors
who used heart balm suits to squeeze money out of male victims.

Legislatures began to think that heart balm laws did more harm than good. Many states enacted anti–heart balm statutes.

Today, heart balm cases are rare and so spiced with salacious sexual and financial details that they make the news. North Carolina is among the few states that retain heart balm laws, and in recent years it has seen some huge damage awards to plaintiffs. In 2019, a CNN headline trumpeted, "A North Carolina Man Just Won a $750,000 Lawsuit after Suing His Wife's Lover." In an earlier North Carolina case, *Hutelmyer v. Cox*, when Mr. Hutelmyer told Mrs. Hutelmyer that he was leaving her for his secretary, she sued the secretary for crim con and alienation of affection, and the outraged jury awarded her a million dollars. Why, laypeople seemed to think, should injuries to the wallet and the body find legal redress, while often far more painful, long-lasting, and life-destroying injuries inflicted in marriages and love relationships have no remedy but divorce? *Hutelmyer* inspired a brief public debate about bringing back heart balm, but lawyers mostly remained negative. The legal scholar Jill Jones records this interchange on *Rivera Live*, CNBC TV, August 11, 1997:

> "Family values," grunted criminal defense attorney Gerald Lefcourt, "this is really absurd, I mean, if it was the law in New York, could you imagine? This whole city would be, like, at the courthouse all the time." Fellow guest and family law attorney Raoul Felder agreed, scorning suits like this as involving "feelings" that should not be allowed to clog up the courts.

The legal echoes of the vow to keep one's spouse retain little of the vow's moral resonance, which rests on the fact that the vow is a vow, taken as the earnest of the couple's love. Although the law, too, enjoins what the vow promises, the law's protection is limited, and the relevant provisions often hide in legal nooks and crannies. A marriage license does little more than create tax, inheritance, and a few divorce rights and duties. When at-will divorce is the law, no matter how dire the material, social, and emotional consequences of marital dissolution, the best that courts can do is to try to divvy property and money fairly and, perhaps, order someone to pay for therapy. Some authorities see this as a grave failing in law, and there's a lot to be said for that view. But it would take a deep dive into the legal waters to judge the ultimate pros and cons. In any case, the point here is something different, and it doesn't depend on who's right about which laws would be best.

On Our Own

The point is to think about where current laws leave us—on our own. The paradoxical effect of this is to make the ancient wedding rite into something more modern and more important. As the law abandons marriage, the demands on people's personal strengths and resources multiply—on their integrity, their capacity for love, their self-knowledge, their ability to take responsibility for the shape of their lives and to determine in the present who they want to be in the future, and to commit to making that happen. When you make the solemn promises of marriage, you need to know how far you can and should trust someone else, and you have to marshal all your inward strengths to figure out whether you can and should ask someone to trust you with their life.

Solemn promises were once the way all significant social and business exchanges and complex, lifelong bonds were established. Promises are still a powerful way to order relationships, and they offer a way of avoiding some of the chaos and anomie of modern life. We're lucky that the culture hasn't forgotten the power of the promise or the solemnity of the vow—and that it hasn't is a fact proven by the very survival of the wedding rite through so many centuries. Promises and vows are a living way to create trust and demonstrate commitment when force and law can't or won't.

This heritage is remarkable because it's not simply something that survived the centuries; it's something that shaped them. It's not easy to find words to express its value that aren't drowned out by the noise and complexities of current politics, cultural and religious conflicts, and the multiple layers of conflicting motives in the history of marriage and its laws. Despite all that, the ideal of marriage embedded in this rite, with its freedom, its encouraging and supportive recognition of human weakness, its call on strength, its implicit affection and respect for the good hearts of people who answer it—all this is human and realistic about the way love works and what will give people their best lives. To make these things lean on the capacity to take responsibility for oneself and the person one loves, in a promise—this is a wise, beautiful thing that emerges from insight into the way love works. It's something you can still believe in, something to aspire to, something that adds significance to your life.

It may be that the law's hard-hearted abandonment of love and marriage has done us a favor. It's a solid fact that the happiest and most stable marriages, overall, are the ones that choose the values set out in the traditional wedding rite, whether couples recite vows or have vow-less Jewish or Eastern Orthodox weddings. In a world where no one is forced into marriage or into any particular kind of marriage, it's harder to pass the buck for failure. It's harder to say that lasting love is an illusion when so many people seem to find it on their own. It's harder to blame laws and conventions for our miseries when laws and conventions leave us to design our own lives. Our era, surprisingly but possibly happily, offers an unprecedented historical teaching moment.

Chapter Eight

NO MATTER WHAT

*"I will love You whatever happens, even though . . ."—there follows a list of catastrophic miracles—(*even though, *I should like to say,* all the stones of Baalbek split into exact quarters, the rooks of Repton utter dire prophecies in Greek and the Windrush bellow imprecations in Hebrew, Time run boustrophedon and Paris and Vienna thrice be lit again by gas . . .)*

Do I believe that these events might conceivably occur during my lifetime? If not, what have I promised? I will love You whatever happens, even though You put on twenty pounds or become afflicted with a moustache: *dare I promise that?*

—W. H. Auden, "Dichtung und Wahrheit
(An Unwritten Poem)" (1960)

With the phrase "for better for worse" a marrying couple promise to perform their vows, no matter how their fortunes change. The phrase is not specific. It's about being steadfast in the marriage—no matter what. When we read it in light of the next words, "for richer for poorer, in sickness and in health," it also seems likely that it is not about what we today would call relationship problems. This entire triad of phrases is about the kinds of troubles and boons that arise from external causes, things that fate throws at us—wars, fires, fame, inheritances, crop failures, unexpected promotions, and so on. Both good and bad fortune, of course, can challenge a relationship.

The triad's second and third pairs of words—"for richer for poorer, in sickness and in health"—focus on two specific kinds of problems that strain a marriage: money and health. "For better for worse" covers everything from a Nobel Prize to the collapse of the stock market, so, logically, these two follow-on promises are superfluous. They read as though they are there to amplify or clarify "for better for worse," or even for stylistic or poetic reasons, to stretch the imagination or enhance meaning with rhythm. But this can't be true because "in sickness and in health" predates the other clauses. It is the oldest specific vow I have been able to find; it occurs in the earliest manuscripts as the sole vow in the ceremony, not one of a triad. For centuries it appeared in different versions of the wedding rite, with different vocabulary and different promises, including one from 1300 in which it was part of a dyad (in old age and in sickness and in health) instead of a triad. With the addition of the second and third specific promises, about money and health, we arrive at the three included in the final version of the marrying sentence ("I take you . . ."). Quarrels about money are among the most common causes of divorce. Illness is a frequent cause of divorce but also among the most egregious of causes; to divorce a spouse because they are ill breaches the vows to keep and to love as well as the specific vow to stand by them in sickness.

The "I take" sentence in one fourteenth-century manuscript of the Sarum rite (quoted in chapter 3) contains all the "no matter what" phrases that made it into the final version:

> Ich .N. take the .N. to my weddyd [wife/housbonde] to hau and
> to holden fro this day forward, for bettere for wers, for richere
> for porere, in seknesse and in helthe [for the woman alone: to
> be boneyre and buxsum in bedde and at borde], tyl deth us
> departe, zif [if] holi cherche hit wyle ordeyne and there to y
> plight the my treuthe.

In the fourteenth century (as chapter 3 explained), "boneyre" and "buxsum"—unlike today's "bonny" and "buxom"—referred to behavior, not appearance. The woman here, but not the man, promised to be pleasant and agreeable in bed—*sexually*, in other words—and at the table. (Going to bed with someone meant the same thing then as now.) Modern attitudes would find these words offensive, and they were deleted long before today's versions appeared. The woman's vows mention bed, but the man's don't. When the man gives her the ring and other gifts, he makes the short solo speech "with my body I thee worship," which is certainly about sex. But it's not a vow, only a gift, and perhaps a declaration of his feelings.

A York manuscript from 1403 has an "I take thee" sentence that is word-for-word identical for men and women, and its three "no matter what" clauses are different from Sarum's, too. York doesn't have "for richer for poorer," and it puts "for better for worse" second, not first.

> [Groom] Here I take ye to my wedded wyfe, to hald and to
> haue at bed and at borde, *for fayrer for layther, for better for wers,*
> *in sekenes and in hele*, till ded us depart, and yare to [thereto] I
> plyght ye my trowth.

[Bride] Here I take ye to my wedded housband, to hald and to haue at bed and at borde, *for fayrer for laythir, for better for wers, in sekenes and in hele,* till dede ws depart, and yare to [thereto] I plyght ye my trowth. (emphasis added)

This wording seems to put more emphasis on sex than the Sarum rite. Both man and woman take the other "to hald and to haue at bed and at borde." Immediately after the mention of bed (and board), the York rite makes a second reference to sex, but this becomes clear only after you figure out that "laythe" means "ugly." Thus, literally, the pair vow to hold and have each other, in bed (as well as at dinner), until death parts them, "for fairer or uglier." This is a promise to maintain a sexual relationship even if one or both decline in physical attractiveness.

You might wonder, as I did, whether we should read the York phrase figuratively. Maybe the phrase "for fayrer for laythir" meant something like "even if 'things' turn ugly." But, in the plain-speaking style of fifteenth-century Yorkshire, it was meant literally: even if *you* turn ugly. To interpret it figuratively would make the phrase redundant with "for better for worse." The literal interpretation is confirmed by other York texts from this period that have the same meaning expressed in a different vocabulary. One of them gives the phrase in even starker Latin that needs no translation: "pulcriori et deformiori." It is a stretch to believe that in this context references to beauty and ugliness are about anything other than sexual attractiveness. The message is that marriage means sex, even if one of you gets wrinkles or goes bald—"for fayrer for laythir." The fact that the phrase "for fayrer for laythir" is *first* in the York triad, before "for better for worse," also suggests the possibility that the couple's sexual relationship is being presented as the heart of the marriage, hence lasting for their lifetimes. (Studies show that people who have been married for fifty or sixty years still have active sex lives.) This impression is reinforced by the awkward placement of "for better for worse" in second position. As the most general of the three phrases, it should come first, or perhaps last, but not in the middle.

It's easier to promise to fight off a shark attack on your mate than to promise to love them after they put on twenty pounds and start wearing mom jeans or grow a mustache after going bald. The first promise is easy because it addresses only your ideals, who you *want* to be and what you *want* to do, not what you think you'll actually be called on to be and do. The second is drearily, scarily realistic about day-to-day life and its power to dull the luster of love—a concern addressed in countless movies, novels, and songs. Virginia Woolf was wise about that dulling in her diary:

> Arnold Bennett says that the horror of marriage lies in its "dai-liness." All acuteness of relationship is rubbed away by this. The truth is more like this: life—say 4 days out of 7—becomes automatic; but on the 5th day a bead of sensation (between husband and wife) forms which is all the fuller and more sensitive because of the automatic customary unconscious days on either side. That is to say the year is marked by moments of great intensity.

If we set out to revise the triad of "no matter what" promises, what might we add or subtract? Given the reality that sometimes marital sexual relationships do fall apart if one or both lose their looks, the 1403 York rite's "for fayrer for layther" was wise then and now. But money problems, too, are up there in the top causes, so Sarum's "for richer for poorer" is also wise. However, if we simply added York's "for fayrer for layther" to the three promises that have come down to us from the Sarum rite, we would make the triad into a quartet of "no matter what"s: "for better for worse, for fairer for layther, for richer for poorer, in sickness and in health." Four are clunky, and any good rite should teach and persuade not only with its ideas but with words that move us by their beauty and rhythm. The "rule of three" governs the way every English speaker hears, reads, and talks the language. We respond with fine-tuned feelings to triplets of words and phrases. Two aren't enough; four are too much.

We would have to eliminate one of the four candidates, but which? "For better for worse"? A bad idea, as it's the clause that covers all the unmentioned bases. "For richer for poorer"? But this one and "for fayrer for layther" may be equally important. True, no one now knows what "layther" means, and "for fairer for uglier" would have the guests snickering. But let's assume that some wordsmith could be called on to phrase it acceptably. We'd then have to consider chucking "in sickness and in health."

This is the oldest, the clearest, and, one supposes, the most likely to be fulfilled. Who is going to run out on a sick or dying mate? The answer to that question depends on why that vow was the first one to be included and why, so far as I can tell, it is the only one that appears in every version of the rite that includes vows. History tells us essentially nothing except the rough dates on which we first find it written down. But we know that for most of history, for most people other than the very rich, an invalid mate was a catastrophic misfortune, and, with rampant smallpox, bubonic plagues, and few medical aids, an appallingly common one.

Although a thousand years ago ordinary people had relatives and friends to turn to, and sometimes clergy or their lord's lady, they depended heavily on their mates. Men were builders, hunters, farmers, butchers, bakers, stonemasons, sailors, soldiers, carpenters, and more. Women were responsible for childbearing and childcare, for the household, cooking, gardening, animal husbandry, nursing and doctoring the sick, growing and preserving herbs for medicines and food, and a variety of essential and sometimes marketable crafts—preserving, weaving, spinning, knitting, sewing. Both sets of skills were essential for survival. A man or woman with an invalid mate (and a child lacking a parent) was not only deprived of love but often endangered. Providing care to a sick, invalid, or dying mate must often have been difficult or impossible given the resources of the household. The temptation to abandon them must have been great, especially if they had a dangerous infection—smallpox or, worst of all, bubonic plague.

Another reason why this specific promise alone shows up in the early wedding rites may have been because it addressed behavior that was regarded as particularly despicable. To refuse to "keep" someone "in sickness" could multiply their sufferings or bring about their death. Leaving a dying person to die alone, after that person has loved you and trusted you, is unspeakably cruel.

These are only guesses. But we may be sure that human nature hasn't changed much since the twelfth century, when this vow appears in the written record. It's still true, especially for the poor, that having an invalid mate is a catastrophic misfortune, and still true that some of the most painful marital failures occur when one spouse deserts the other "in sickness" or at death's door. As for how often things like this happen today, we needn't rely on guesswork.

A 2009 study addressed the effect of life-threatening illness on marriages in a group of 515 patients. The patients had been referred to neuro-oncology clinics in several states, and the study was carried out by an oncologist, neurologists, and experts in biostatistics and epidemiology, all of whom were affiliated with universities or clinics. The patients were all married; 254 were women, and 261 were men. The study found that most of the patients' mates stood by them throughout their illness, but a substantial minority did not. Sadly, more men than women fell short when their mate was seriously ill. The overall rate of divorce and separation in the research group was the same as in the general population, but this statistic concealed a troubling truth: women in the study were *less* likely to separate from or divorce husbands who were seriously ill, but men were *more* likely to divorce or separate from wives who were seriously ill. Overall, the rate of abandonment among couples facing serious illness was similar to that among couples without serious illness. But seriously ill women faced a staggering *sixfold increase* (20.8 percent, up from 2.9 percent) in the rate of abandonment. Of the 515 marriages, sixty (11.6 percent of them) ended in divorce or separation within six months after the patient's diagnosis of serious illness. The woman was the abandoned party in 88 percent of these sixty cases, and abandonment was more likely if a woman suffered from "neurobehavioral changes."

As one would expect, those abandoned mates were less likely to complete their medical treatment, to be involved in clinical trials, or to be able to die at home. Surely they faced more difficulties with the quotidian troubles of filling and following prescriptions, and of managing transportation, money, shopping, housekeeping, personal care, and nutrition. They also likely endured greater discouragement, depression, and despair.

Most men, like most women, stuck by their suffering mates, and the longer they had been married, the more likely they were to do so. The authors of this study do not explain their results and only point out that some studies suggest "that men are less able to undertake a caregiving role and assume the burdens of home and family maintenance compared with women"—something we didn't need a crew of neurologists, biostatisticians, and oncologists to tell us.

Yet those who abandon a seriously ill mate may themselves be suffering. Emotionally speaking, they may be coming apart or facing a breakdown. Caretaking can be brutally hard work under emotionally devastating circumstances. Some people experience a spouse's serious illness as abandonment; they may become angry or feel unloved or in danger. Community support may be thin or absent when it's desperately needed. To come through for someone in these circumstances is to survive a test of love that requires strength and courage.

A promise—in sickness and in health—that lays a foundation for a shared future life is in itself a resource for the future. Would I come through for a mate who is seriously ill or dying? Does my answer have anything to do with whether I promised to five years or five decades ago, wearing my wedding finery? The answer is clear in a moving op-ed in the *New York Times* by Tom Coughlin, an NFL Super Bowl–winning coach, about the four years he had spent nursing a beloved wife. She "has been everything to our family," but now was dying of a brain disorder that slowly eroded her ability to walk, speak, think, or remember:

> I've learned firsthand caregiving is all-consuming. It is mentally and physically exhausting. Sometimes you just need a break. When Judy is having a good day, then my day is good. But then there are dark days—those days that are so full of frustration and anger, they have me feeling like a failure and pondering the unfairness of the disease. I've spent my entire life preparing for some of the biggest games a person could play, but nothing can prepare you to be a caregiver who has to watch a loved one slip away.
>
> I am not seeking sympathy. It's the last thing I want. It's the last thing most caregivers want. Taking care of Judy is a promise I made 54 years ago when she was crazy enough to say "I do."

Chapter Nine

FIDELITY AND ITS DISCONTENTS

What he didn't understand was why there should be all this fuss about such
a simple thing as love-making . . .

"So what?" replied the clerk. "Everybody does it in Paris."
And this remark, like an irresistible argument, decided her.

—Gustave Flaubert,
Madame Bovary (1857), my translation

The promise to forsake all others is a promise not to have sex with other people. It's not about office flirtations, extramarital lunches enlivened by romantic sparks, or even full-fledged online-only affairs. Although those things violate other vows, in this chapter "infidelity" means adultery: sex acts. From the beginning, the church called for exclusive marital relations, but the vow of fidelity does not appear in the marriage rite, so far as I have seen, until the fourteenth century, and is reliably included only in the mid-sixteenth century.

The sexual revolutions of the past half century, along with

decades of experiments in swinging, open, polyamorous, communal, and other plural sexual relationships, have contributed to mistrust and rejection of the vow of fidelity. Doubts about it reflect the frequency with which it gets breached, the desire to breach it, the fear of being unable to keep it, and the suspicion that breaching it wouldn't or shouldn't be very terrible. Some couples now omit "forsaking all others" from their wedding vows. Some choose to cohabit instead of marrying. Meanwhile, long after the countercultural love-life experiments of the sixties, seventies, and eighties ended in disillusionment or indifference, writers at high-end publications have begun to opine that various forms of consensual nonmonogamy (CNM) are tomorrow's normal. It's a view that doesn't quite fit with some other facts.

For example, polls show that although the vow of fidelity is widely questioned and adultery laws are mostly gone, mores have hardly budged. A 2022 Gallup poll found that a whopping 89 percent of Americans think it is morally wrong for married people to have affairs. Another survey found the same attitudes toward all "committed" relationships, not only marriages: "eighty-six percent of respondents said that *committed* couples should be monogamous (sixty-four percent "strongly agree[d]") and eighty-nine percent would not consider an open sexual relationship" (emphasis added). Surveys also suggest that nonetheless something like 13 percent of married women and 20 percent of married men commit adultery, which proves that some among the 89 percent who think it's wrong do it anyway. But this is true of everything that's wrong—cheating at golf, slandering, lying, stealing, and murdering. Everyone does things that they regard as wrong, whether shockingly or only head-shakingly so. In no other case is this fact treated as evidence that the conduct in question isn't really harmful or wrong or should be legitimated; or that it's too much to ask of people; or that I can't trust *myself* not to do it since so many other men and women can't.

It's Nothing New

Those who reject monogamous fidelity often describe it as a remnant of some dying heritage—Christian, puritanical, Victorian, or other oppressive and outmoded mentality. But marital fidelity was cherished and admired thousands of years before any of those traditions existed. In fact, if you want to read a rip-roaringly good story about an admirable, lovable, and honorable husband and wife dealing with people who want to tempt them from their mates, read *The Odyssey*. Again.

My husband, E, an English professor, got what he took for unexpected proof of its power when he was invited to give two lectures on classical works at a distant university. He flew there on the day of the first lecture and was met at the airport by a literary couple, Hannah and Harold, who, all smiles, took him to lunch. Harold was going to do the introductory honors at the first lecture and Hannah at the second. The three of them had the kind of conversation that three English professors would consider quite lively, and then drove to E's hotel. Later that afternoon, E made his way to the lecture hall, where Harold took the podium, explained the lecture series to the roomful of scholars and students, and concluded with an enthusiastic introduction for E.

E's lecture touched movingly on the marriage of Penelope and Odysseus—on Penelope's steadfastness and her cleverness, and Homer's, too, in the way he used hers to display the inner qualities of their marriage. In the final scene, Odysseus has at last returned home, after resisting—not entirely successfully—liaisons with two goddesses, first Circe and then Calypso. Both goddesses used their supernatural powers to compel him to have sex. Somewhat huffily, Calypso tried to talk him out of his longing to go home to Penelope:

> Can I be less desirable than she is?
> Less interesting? Less beautiful? Can mortals
> compare with goddesses in grace and form?

Odysseus responds diplomatically that he's well aware that a goddess is superior to Penelope in all these ways, yet he can't help longing for the human woman, who will grow old and die. On his next stop, he is equally courteous but evasive with a king's daughter, who is beautiful—and wild for him—but he isn't tempted.

Meanwhile, by means of deception, Penelope has managed to hold off a crowd of greedy suitors, who want her to pick one of them to marry so as to usurp Odysseus's position. They're certain that Odysseus, absent without word for nearly twenty years, is dead. In Penelope's immense loyalty and love for Odysseus, she, too, has been faithful all those years. When Odysseus arrives, incognito, she makes a show of not recognizing him. Yet she meets and subtly strategizes with this supposed stranger on how to deal with the dangerous crowd of suitors. After he fights and kills them all (they *were* after his wife), Homer gives us a delicious scene, *in their bedroom*, initially in the presence of their son, Telemachus, who protests her refusal to recognize his father. After Telemachus leaves, Penelope tells Odysseus's aged nurse to move the marriage bed over to the wall, and Odysseus is furious. He knows the bed can't be moved without destroying it, as he himself carved one of its bedposts out of an olive tree still rooted in the ground. Now, having made him prove his identity *and* display how he treasures their sexual relationship—in his angry protectiveness of their marriage bed—Penelope cries out to him, "Do not rage at me, Odysseus," and rushes into his arms.

It's better when Homer tells it. But the point comes through even in a plot summary of this nearly three-thousand-year-old story. Love between husband and wife is depicted as strong, permanent, sexual, exclusive, and admirable. Not only that, but kids passionately want their parents to stick together, and shouldn't be in the room when they're talking about sex and beds. No law or church or fear of what people might say, only their love, compelled Penelope and Odysseus to feel and act as they did.

But the real-life twenty-first-century story of Harold, Hannah, and E didn't end there. The audience evidently enjoyed the talk, and E enjoyed the discussion afterward. The following week, as E readied his second lecture, he was happily looking forward to repeating the fun. This time, when he arrived at the airport, only Harold was there to greet him, and he was in low spirits. Hannah wasn't feeling well, he said, and wouldn't be able to introduce him at the second lecture. Talk dragged during lunch and on the drive to E's hotel. Harold and Hannah were both absent from the lecture that afternoon, and a stranger made introductory remarks that were obviously prepared in haste. E worried that Hannah was very sick. Though the audience listened attentively, the whole second occasion lacked the spark of the first.

In his hotel room that night, E felt a bit down and, still worried about Hannah, he fired off a short email to her, hoping that she was feeling better. She sent a reply at five in the morning. When he read it over breakfast, E gasped in dismay and clutched his head. She wasn't sick at all, it turned out. As her email explained, she'd been too upset to attend the lecture because she had suddenly decided to end her decades-long marriage. E realized that his lecture must have hit Hannah hard. She reported that Harold had been having an affair for years. She'd long suspected it but had preferred not to face it. The trigger for confronting things, E inferred, was hearing his own discussion of Odysseus's and Penelope's steadfast love and faithfulness.

Unexpected Consequences of Infidelity

Infidelity, not consensual nonmonogamy, continues to be the most common form of rebellion against ancient marital values and one of the top two causes of divorce in the United States. In a recent study, 60 percent of divorcing couples cited infidelity as the cause. The only factor more common than infidelity was a vague "lack of commitment," which seems to overlap with infidelity; it was cited in 75 percent of cases. A well-known 1989 study by an anthropologist and historian, Laura Betzig, examined causes of divorce worldwide, past and present. The most common cause, by a strong margin, was infidelity. The tendency to believe that casual adultery is not a big deal leads a surprising number of people to engage in it or profess tolerant attitudes toward it—until it happens to them. Then the trauma resulting from even a casual one-night stand, let alone a passionate, ongoing relationship, comes as a devastating shock to the betrayed partner and, very often, to the adulterer, too.

The psychologist Judith Wallerstein conducted a study in which she asked happily married couples, among other things, what would break their marriage. Many responded that they would be tolerant of casual infidelity—say a one-night stand on a lonely business trip. They wouldn't like it, but they would forgive it. But it turned out that people's actual reactions weren't what they had expected. "One woman cried for two years after discovering that her husband had spent one night with another woman . . . Despite their claims of open-mindedness and acceptance of infidelity, people who were cheated on were shocked and miserable, even if it was only a one-night stand."

Wallerstein was not arguing for divorcing unfaithful spouses. She was trying to explain a painful reality to those who lacked personal experience of it. Infidelity creates grief, pain, and rage that, on an emotional Richter scale, is on a par with the experience of loss in death, and some people say that it's worse. The betrayed spouse or lover may be simultaneously enraged, despairing, and frightened—of abandonment by the mate or loss of their esteem and affection, destruction of their home and family, misery for their children. The stress level is extreme, and comes with major depression and debilitating anxiety. A number of studies show that infidelity in both married and cohabiting couples can also lead to physical consequences—venereal disease being the most obvious. People who experience a mate's infidelity may undergo extreme stress, and often show many of the same symptoms of post-traumatic stress as soldiers who have been in combat, with a similar array of mental and physical disturbances and a similar vulnerability to disease and other physical disorders. For these and other reasons, victims of infidelity get sick and die more often than people in solid relationships. Anxiety and depression can cause decreased immune function and inflammation, which may be associated with heart disease, diabetes, metabolic syndrome, and other conditions. One study concluded that marital quality had a substantially stronger effect on heart-failure patients' rates of death (from all causes) than other factors often cited in "the broader behavioral cardiology literature," such as the patient's level of optimism or hostility or their social support. Stress cardiomyopathy, a dangerous condition caused by extreme emotional or physical stress, is commonly known, for obvious reasons, as "broken heart syndrome." And, of course, the enormous distress over such betrayals is a common cause of assault, suicide, and murder.

Some research points to infidelity as a significant cause of cardiovascular problems in both betrayed persons and betrayers. Men engaged in adulterous sex seem to be significantly more likely to die in the act than men having sex with their wives. The studies suggest that this may be a result of their being overexcited, trying too hard, drinking or eating too much beforehand, or working too hard to keep up with a much younger lover, as allegedly happened to New York governor Nelson Rockefeller. One study on the frequency of death while cheating suggests that a guilty conscience may contribute to the strain, and hence to the increased cardio-vascular risk.

When divorce follows infidelity, betrayed spouses are less likely to adjust well than those whose divorces stemmed from other causes. Many are never the same afterward, even if they manage to reconcile with their spouse or go on to a happier relationship. Betrayed partners may brave it out admirably, adjusting to divorce and turning their lives around. They manage the stiff upper lip and sincerely utter the usual words of acceptance, "It's for the best." But no one ever says that, while the divorce hurt a lot, the whole experience was one they are glad they didn't miss out on. Everyone wishes the marriage had either never foundered or never happened, even while they treasure its children, whom they wish they had instead found under a cabbage leaf.

Given the emotional and physical costs of infidelity, why isn't some form of consensual nonmonogamy a logical alternative to exclusive marital relations? Why not broaden personal choice to encompass polyamory or open marriage or what still get called "swinging" marriages and relationships? All propose an ethical way to lead a plural love life, one that rests on honesty, full consent, and equal respect and rights for men and women. Wouldn't most or all of the Sturm und Drang of adulterous marriages be prevented in committed relationships with no expectations of sexual fidelity?

Among the illustrious past defenders of these ideas are a world-famous philosopher, Bertrand Russell, and an immortal poet, Percy Bysshe Shelley. In 1929, Russell wrote a sharp critique of monogamous marriage. He argued that the people who value love most are also going to be those who find marital fidelity most difficult because marriage makes love into a duty. To make it a duty "to love so-and-so is the surest way to cause you to hate him or her. Marriage as a combination of love with legal bonds thus falls between two stools." His argument would also apply to monogamous cohabitation—the combination of love with only moral bonds, no legal ones, which is so often the practical situation today. Russell quoted Shelley's *Epipsychidion* (1821), a poetic critique of marriage and celebration of free love:

> I was never attached to that great sect
> Whose doctrine is, that each one should select
> Out of the crowd a mistress or a friend,
> And all the rest, though fair and wise, commend
> To cold oblivion, though it is in the code
> Of modern morals and the beaten road
>   . . . and so
> With one chained friend, perhaps a jealous foe,
> The dreariest and the longest journey go.

Russell argued that marriage, by closing off new love, "diminish[es] receptivity and sympathy and the opportunities of valuable human contacts. It is to do violence to something which, from the most idealistic standpoint, is in itself desirable." Marriage, he said, by killing love with obligatory fidelity, creates a morally faulty relationship. Today's proponents of open marriage agree, and, they add, really loving someone obligates us to cultivate the ability to feel "compersion" for our loved one's happiness in someone else's arms—to be happy for them. ("Compersion" is a term coined by members of the Kerista commune. It has been picked up by academicians writing on the ethics of plural love but isn't yet in dictionaries, though it's been in use for decades.) And if *you* gain happiness and *your spouse* gains happiness, what's not to like? Thus, they conclude, with Russell, that not only is monogamy morally not obligatory but that it's morally good to spread love around—though, of course, many people lack the personal and moral resources to live by these higher values.

Shelley and Russell and other writers propose, in effect, that we *retrain* the kind of love that leads people to marry so as to keep its joys and satisfactions while sharing it with multiple others. But, as contemporary defenders of consensual nonmonogamy teach, this isn't easy. Jealousy and other conflicts arising from plural loyalties are the plague of CNM relationships. CNM also requires an ability actually to *want* new lovers even though you love the one you're with. How did Russell and Shelley handle such problems?

Shelley married twice (he died at age twenty-nine), and Russell married four times. They both had affairs. Both men's pursuit of love resulted in a string of broken hearts and estranged or abandoned children. Shelley's first marriage was a teenage elopement that ended with his young wife's suicide after he left her for Mary Wollstonecraft Godwin. He married the extraordinary Mary, and they had an open marriage. As often happens in open marriages, though both agreed in principle on free love, only Shelley actually exercised the freedom, and his doing so left Mary wretched and angry despite her views.

During Bertrand Russell's second marriage, which was by mutual agreement an open marriage, Russell was made so intolerably miserable by his wife's extramarital liaisons that he recanted. He not only publicly repudiated his notorious defense of open marriage, but more than once insisted that it was all her idea. Both he and his wife had multiple extramarital affairs, and their marriage ended with a prolonged, acrimonious divorce and fierce custody battles that made their children wretched. Russell then married the woman with whom he was having his current affair (an Oxford undergraduate at its outset, when Russell was in his early sixties). That marriage, too, ended bitterly. At the age of eighty, he married again, and this fourth marriage was happy, loving, and faithful until his death at ninety-seven. Russell wrote in his *Autobiography*:

> In my second marriage, I had tried to preserve that respect
> for my wife's liberty which I thought that my creed enjoined.
> I found, however, that my capacity for forgiveness and what
> may be called Christian love was not equal to the demands
> that I was making on it, and that persistence in a hopeless
> endeavor would do much harm to me, while not achieving the
> intended good to others. Anybody else could have told me this
> in advance, but I was blinded by theory.

It's important to understand that for Russell and Shelley and their wives, "free love" didn't mean mere consensual extramarital sex. The free love they aspired to was sexual love for whole cherished and adored persons. The problem with "freeing" that kind of love is that love like that typically centers on one person and sticks stubbornly to that person. Once a marriage forms around such love, it is likely to last forever, monogamously, because that kind of love is also jealous. Many of those who experiment with consensual nonmonogamy discover this when they happen upon real love and find themselves tormented by jealousy and caught in conflict. Because attempts at finding plural love—*real* love, not simply sex—so often don't work out, people with open relationships today typically aspire only to *sexually* open relationships and try to avoid falling in love. They bow to the likelihood of a breakup should either of them fall in love with someone other than their partner.

Polyamory

The term "polyamory" is usually reserved for plural relations that are genuine love relations, and true polyamory aims at an ambitious goal: real love relations on an ethical basis of open-ness and acceptance. Compared to relationships open only to sexual encounters, polyamory's potential for conflicts, jealousy, and instability in the relationships, especially if the arrange-ment involves shared living spaces, increases exponentially—over interference with one's own children, caring for others' children, money, the best bedroom, privacy rules, whose turn it is for sex, and who ate all the Oreo Double Stufs. Whether the arrangement involves shared or separate households, the heightened potential for jealousy and conflict leads to intense focus on figuring out how to make things work. The accepted solution both for sexually open marriages and polyamory is to make rules and follow them.

Lists of them are posted on the internet. Rulemaking may require meetings and votes. The rules, or codes of conduct, stress the need for frequent communication and for "transparency," and provide moral instruction on how to share love and lovers, and feel "compersion" for your beloved's happiness in loving (sexually) someone else. They also address where, when, and how often you can meet with a lover or have one move in, or move out yourself; what you should and shouldn't tell each of your loves; and, with shared living spaces, all the rules of the house about cooking, cleaning, bills, noise, and so on.

Even the least complicated forms of polyamory—say, a primary California couple, in which one has a second love partner in Cleveland—will to some extent interfere with marital privacy. If that second person really is loved, to some extent, directly or indirectly, both primary partners have to share the most private parts of their life with the third beloved partner. If your mate's other beloved(s) lose their job or develop a debilitating illness, this is going to require action on your mate's part—and will seriously affect your life. In larger polyamorous groups, the internal affairs of a relationship to some degree *must* be a matter of general or public discussion and negotiation. Your relationship no longer is just between the two of you. This loss of privacy, in turn, undermines your freedom to be, say, and do what no one else can know or judge when the two of you are alone. (Recall that Penelope and Odysseus reconnected through their shared secret.) Your intimate life is exposed to others' judgment, control, criticism, and even ridicule. CNM, by its nature, makes sexual relations quasi-public, which is what some people prefer. The tradeoff for this is a much higher level of constraint on intimate life than in exclusive marriages.

An Unsung Joy of Marriage

CNM's very nature as plural requires sacrifice of one of the most treasured, enchanting, and least discussed aspects of married life: its luxurious, protective privacy and the oxygen of freedom it generates. That freedom is itself a joy, and it brings a cascade of other good things in its wake. The outer social world recedes yet comes into truer focus as a couple share and discuss their observations, in the privileged privacy of marriage. Trivial concerns are aired; the humor triggered by intimacy emerges, with teasing and private jokes. For a convincing fictional description of how this sort of interchange is both light and deep, and simultaneously about us and ours, here and now, and other people and distant events, see how Hilary Mantel imagines private moments between Thomas Cromwell and his beloved wife, Liz, in *Wolf Hall*. Their conversation is intermixed with his thoughts in a way that is true to real married experience. The talk and thoughts wander from domestic matters to the king's dangerous wishes to annul his marriage to their relatives to religion, their son, her work, the dog, a friend's trouble, and still more. His affection for her is never mentioned or named, but this scene from a marriage fills you with it, and makes you mourn for her with him when she dies.

In modern monogamous marriage, the couple's special devotion to each other creates a private two-person realm where the rules of social life don't apply and the social group itself is shut out. Relaxation is the result. The experience of *sharing* that relaxation of your guard in privacy and in physical intimacy belongs to the domain of love. It releases powerful feelings of many kinds, from passion to peace—or anger. Parts of yourself that are suppressed in public and on the job reemerge in marital privacy. In their private times, couples enjoy freedom from countless indispensable, sensible rules that operate automatically in social settings and dictate what you can say; establish formalities of greeting and parting; forbid certain kinds of clothing and unclothing, various kinds of public display, loud singing, talking in the theater, and gossiping; or require you to hide your feelings or to show respect when you feel none. (Of course, laws and moral values operate even inside marital privacy—against violence, cruelty, abuse, lies, and so on.) In marital privacy, you can drop your front, tell each other secrets that no one else can know, and say and do a thousand things that can't be said and done around others. The most secret and private of all is the freedom to offer each other special care and attention and appreciation, and, of course, enjoy a sexual relationship that for most people is eminently satisfactory. What's not to dislike—when you're not one of them?

As a happily married friend once cautioned a newly married and bubbling-over acquaintance who was sharing her glow about how delightful it is to be married, "Yes, but you know you can't say this to anyone." She meant that you can't tell other people how in the privacy of married life you experience this delightful lightness of being. No one wants to hear about it, which means that some of the best news there is about marriage gets treated like a state secret. In public, married people speak with a traditional sarcastic tolerance about the person they love so much they're ready to die for them. If they didn't attitudinize like this, even their friends would hate them. Even many of their happily married friends would hate them.

Western-style monogamy, with its equal genders and social freedoms, is an institution honed into workability and high satisfaction over a few millennia of trial and error and insight-gathering. The wedding rite's vow of fidelity goes to the heart of what makes it work: the choice of one person to love and share life with. Of course, it doesn't always work. Some marriages are miserable, and divorces are frequent. But marriage doesn't have to be fail-safe to be far superior to the alternatives. To abandon the ancient rite's vow of fidelity is to revise for the worse the world's best blueprint for happiness.

Chapter Ten

LOVE AGAINST DEATH

"What now?" she asked me, as we lay together in her bed . . .

"For us?" I said.

"Yeah, for us."

"What do you want?"

"What do you want?"

"I want you and me to be together."

"Married?"

"Not married, unless that really matters to you."

"It doesn't."

"Okay. Me neither. But back together. You and me. And I will be faithful. I swear to you, El. No more . . . anybody else. Come and live with me."

"And be your love?"

"And be my love, for ever."

"Till death do us part?"

"Yes. So?"

"Children?"

"Eh? Oh, absolutely. Well?"

—Iain Banks, *Stonemouth* (2012)

Years earlier, the couple in this vignette had broken up on the eve of their wedding because the man was unfaithful. All is forgiven, but the two of them seem to have the idea that what went wrong before was their plan to have a wedding. Yet in this scene they are taking private vows to love and be faithful and live together (share bed and board) and have babies—*till death do them part*. Although they say they don't care about marriage, the author is going out of his way to make clear that they actually intend to have a marriage—and not an unconventional type of marriage either. They want the kind of marriage created by the traditional vows. What they clearly don't want is receptions, officiants, flowers, rehearsals, rehearsal dinners, fancy clothes, showers, bachelor parties—all the rigmarole of modern weddings. Whether they will march down to the appropriate office and get a marriage license is unclear, but I'd guess the answer is no. Even so, this scene is actually a wedding, creating an informal marriage, and readers are the guest witnesses to their promises. Yet it would have sounded like plans for serial monogamy or cohabitation, not like plans for marriage, if they hadn't added the clincher: "till death do us part."

The solemn moment in a wedding when the couple take vows is usually the point when guests start to tear up and cry. But not all vows inspire that reaction. If the vows are funny or noncommittal or maturely acknowledge that some marriages don't work out though the two of them really hope theirs will, there will be smiles and good wishes, but no tears. What induces the crying is the poignancy of the traditional promises, which are poignant no matter what words people use to make them—as Iain Banks demonstrates with two people talking in bed.

The marriage vows didn't fully acquire this tone until Thomas Cranmer tweaked them. (I've already discussed Cranmer's secret marriage and his long preoccupation with the nature of the institution in chapter 4.) The phrase "til death us departe" had been in the rite for at least two centuries before Cranmer. The twelfth-century Magdalen Pontifical, in which the couple vow "in sickness and in health," does not have the phrase "till dethe us departe." But it begins to show up in the marrying sentences in fourteenth-century manuscripts—here from a Sarum (Salisbury Cathedral) manual that already has most of the words that are still in the Anglican Book of Common Prayer's matrimonial ceremony (plus the unwelcome parts that were eventually dropped):

> Ich .N. take the .N. to my weddyd housbonde to hau and to
> holden fro this day forward, for bettere, for wers, for richere for
> porere, in seknesse and in helthe to be boneyre and buxsum in
> bedde and at borde, *tyl deth us departe,* zif [if] holi cherche hit wyle
> ordeyne and there to y plight the my treuthe. (emphasis added)

The phrase also occurs in a fifteenth-century Welsh manual's marrying sentence: "forte deth us departe"; and in Latin in a fifteenth-century York manuscript, "quosque mors nos separauerit."

A fourteenth-century York manuscript has a gentler phrase, but in the consents, not in the marrying sentence. The priest asks:

> N. wyll yow have this man to thi husband and to be bwxum
> to hym, luf hym, obeye to hym, and wirschipe hym, serue him
> and kepe hym in hele and in seknes and in all other degrese,
> be to hym als a wyff suld be to hir husband and all othere to

forsake for hym, and hald the onely to hym *tyll thi lyues ende*.

[She is to answer:] I will. (emphasis added)

Compared with "till death do us part," "tyll thi lyues ende" is a more positive, reassuring thought. To tell someone "I'll love you my whole life" will induce a smile. Only the couple's parents might be brought to tears by those softer words, because they remind parents that their child has grown up and is leaving them—and has replaced them. But vows that inspire thoughts about how death will one day tear them apart raise far different emotions. Those words can make even third cousins and new housemates tear up, and, of course, the couple themselves. Death might come at any time, moreover, and no one escapes.

Love, too, was entirely absent in the oldest manuscripts. Love of some sort finally shows up in the consents in fourteenth-century and fifteenth-century texts—when "till death us do part" also begins to appear. But the love mentioned there may not be the "cherishing" kind, and while it appears only in the consents, death is mentioned only in the marrying sentence. Love and death come at separate times and in separate thoughts of the rite.

Love and death first come together in the same sentence—the marrying sentence—in Cranmer's 1549 Book of Common Prayer. Before this, although the marriage rite had made marriage lifelong, it had never explicitly contraposed death and the tender love of marriage. It was left to a prose master, Cranmer, to add that small, powerful twist to the rite. The cherishing love that Cranmer added, moreover, was a kind that can be destroyed, though not easily and always with great pain, and otherwise ends only in death.

It is this combination of "till dethe us departe" with "love and cherishe" that makes the vows poignant. It inspires emotions that release tears because it makes us feel how love triumphs over death and how, without love, death's shadow darkens all of life. Love lives in many places, not only marriage, but marriage is one of its richest, happiest homes. It's the one with the fullest sexual dimension, and it's the one that is open to everyone and most surely provides "the mutuall societe, helpe, and coumforte" that human beings need to flourish. The words of the vows remind us that a young couple now basking in the exhilaration of their love and their wedding will have to face hard things, including their own mortality. But they will have love to sustain their courage and cheerfulness.

A True Story from Our Times

While I was writing this chapter, I described it to a recently married young woman who responded with a thoughtful silence, and then surprised me with a true-life story about a college friend of hers. This friend was diagnosed with a fatal form of brain cancer. She fought valiantly to live and, in the course of her struggles, she and her oncologist, having apparently fallen in love, married. They were not long married when the treatments that failed everyone else unexpectedly worked for her, and miraculously she was cured. A few years later she remains cured and is cheerfully leading a life busy with friends, work, and travel plans. The marriage, however, did not long outlast the illness. It's easy to see how she would have fallen for the man working desperately to save her life against seemingly insuperable odds—though believing that, at best, he could only help prolong it for some months—and how that man's concern for her could have led him to fall for her. But if they had vowed to stay together until death parted them, they breached the vow soon after they concluded that she was not dying. What they had together, briefly, was beautiful and loving, but it wasn't marital love. It was not based on the wish to spend their lives together, but on a wish to face her imminent death together.

Two Surprisingly Cheerful Ancient Fairy Tales

When Cranmer wrote "love" into the marrying sentence, he did so out of his own experience in a secret, forbidden marriage, which exposed him and his family to a constant threat of discovery and harm. Yet clearly, as he revises the old rite, he is not regretting his own dangerous marital choices but doubling down on them. He reminds his contemporaries—and us—of truths that are easily forgotten or undervalued. Humankind had understood them in far more ancient times.

Contrast the relationship between the young student and her doctor with Odysseus and Penelope's, when Odysseus was still held prisoner by Calypso. Calypso tells Odysseus that if he knew what was in store for him, he would stay with her and *become immortal, escape death*, and forget all about "that bride for whom you pine each day."

To this the strategist Odysseus answered:
"My lady goddess, here is no cause for anger.
My quiet Penelope—how well I know—
would seem a shade before your majesty,
death and old age being unknown to you,
while she must die."

He is called "the strategist" here because he is "handling" Calypso, with her jealousy and anger and dangerous supernatural powers. He has to avoid praising Penelope and downplay his yearning for her.

Odysseus not only prefers the mortal woman, but in order to be with her he actually turns down an offer of immortality. He wants to spend his life with Penelope and grow old and die together. Homer's story is a startlingly clear affirmation of love's power over the fear of death. The story about the young woman, the oncologist, and their brief marriage typically elicits gasps of relief, smiles, and much well-wishing. But it isn't a story about finding someone you love so much that you want to spend your life with them.

The other happy tale is Ovid's, from the year 8. It is almost the opposite of the tale of the patient and the oncologist. It's about a couple in old age who have been together all their lives and still love each other very much. They have had what Odysseus and Penelope will, we hope, go on to experience. Ovid's tale also makes the point that wealth, power, and status are not preconditions for this kind of happiness, a point that strangely enough is usually made only in fairy tales, although it is an easily observed truth. Disguised as mortals, Jupiter and Mercury arrive in Phrygia and knock at a thousand doors asking for shelter and rest, but "a thousand doors were bolted against them." Finally they come to a humble cottage with a straw roof where live Baucis and Philemon, a kindly elderly couple who welcome the weary travelers and invite them in. Ovid carefully details the signs of poverty inside the hut—the worn furnishings, the rickety little three-legged table, and a ceiling so low that the tall gods must stoop to enter. Despite their poverty Baucis and Philemon consult and come up with a good meal (including cream cheese and eggs "very lightly cooked on a moderate ash heat") that reduces their spare provisions to one terrified goose, which the two gods won't let them kill and roast. Meanwhile, their small vessel of wine begins mysteriously to refill itself when it should have been long emptied. This, eventually, is the tip-off to the couple that they are entertaining immortals.

Naturally, the gods are delighted by such generosity to apparently needy strangers. As they leave, they punish all the people in the thousand households who refused them hospitality by drowning them in their houses, saving only Baucis and Philemon from that fate, and they turn the old couple's rough hut into a splendid temple with noble columns, a gilded roof, and marble pavements. And, as all supernatural beings in fairy tales do, they reward the old couple's kindness by granting them a wish:

> At last King Jupiter gently addressed them: "You good old man, and you the wife that his goodness deserves, now name whatever boon you desire." Philemon conferred for a moment with Baucis, before advising the gods of their joint decision: "We ask to be priests and to guard your temple; and since we have passed our years

together in peace, let the same hour carry us off, so I need not
look on my dear wife's grave, nor she have to bury my body."
Their wish was granted; as long as life was allowed them, they served
as the temple's guardians. When time had taken its final toll,
and while they were casually standing in front of the steps of the
   building,
telling the sanctuary's history, both Philemon and Baucis
witnessed their partner sprouting leaves on their worn old limbs.
As the tops of the trees spread over their faces, they spoke to
   each other
once more while they could. "Farewell, my beloved!" they said
   in a single
breath, as the bark closed over their lips and concealed them
   for ever.
Still to this day the peasants of Phrygia point to the oak
and the linden nearby which once were the forms of Philemon
   and Baucis.

The gods can't prevent death from separating them, for they are
mere mortals. But they can spare them the pain of being separated.
Baucis and Philemon say "farewell" and are transformed at the
same moment.

Ovid's story makes us aware that current attitudes toward
age are different from Jupiter's and Mercury's affectionate and
respectful ones. It suggests that those who view old age negatively will not readily think happy thoughts about growing old side
by side with someone they love. Fear and loathing of age, when
age is viewed entirely as an unwelcome reminder of decline and

mortality, undercuts the capacity to love. To be able to imagine loving someone until death do you part requires being able to imagine loving someone old and being loved oneself in age. It means that you have to be able to see old people as "us," not some foreign "them." Ovid's elderly couple are very poor and old, but they're not "retired" and don't live the segregated lives of the aged in our own day. They are generous, kind, competent, and good company even for gods. Jupiter and Mercury see that although the pair work hard to provide food and shelter for themselves, they share both unstintingly with strangers. When offered a reward they do not choose wealth or idleness but ask for work—guarding the temple, and, it seems, they are busily doing just that on the day they die.

A loving marriage is the best defense people have against the fear of death and, for the bereaved survivor, its consequences in loneliness, poverty, or other misfortunes. It supports longevity, mental health, financial security, and happiness both for the couple and their children. These and other practical benefits of getting married and growing old together are regularly trumpeted in the press. There are also benefits that get less public attention but are equally important, and may contribute to the practical goods just listed.

A long, affectionate marriage means that you have someone in your life who not only knows your story but is part of it. The two of you develop a bank of shared memories that you continue to add to, filling it with everything important that has happened to the two of you, along with smaller treasures of memory, little things that no one else knows about or values but that you revisit over and over, alone or with your spouse—moments, remarks, events that are stars of meaning by which you navigate your shared future lives. The loss of this is one of the devastating effects of divorce.

When adulthood begins to be measured in plural decades, your shared life becomes a larger and larger part of who you are, and gives a welcome weight to your existence. The single life has many advantages, too, but my own experience of being single was that years of unshared life left me vulnerable to feeling lonely and weightless. Falling asleep at night, I often had the feeling of floating off into the stratosphere, as though my life was too light-weight to anchor me to the earth. For most of us, life only has the weight it needs to ground us if we have someone in our life who cares very much about us, and for whom we care very much, and the time-honored way of achieving this, one honed and shaped by millennia into a highly functional form for living, is marriage.

Married love is what humankind brought with them out of paradise, a gift—whether of nature or, as Cranmer says, of God, or both, all the same a gift. Shared love gives courage and lets us experience our lives as boundless and infinite, though we all know very well how short a lifetime is. Shared love is how we mortals live with joy in the face of death.

III

The Social Life of Love

Chapter Eleven

LOVE AND MONOGAMY:
THE WORLD THEY MAKE

The sociable interest is by its nature diffused: even the maternal feeling admits of plurality of objects; revenge does not desire to have but one victim; the love of domination needs many subjects; but the greatest intensity of love limits the regards to one.

—Alexander Bain, *The Emotions and the Will* (1876)

W hen two people love each other, they almost always want an exclusive, permanent relationship—monogamy. From a social point of view, even monogamy's built-in downsides (giving up an uncharted future and the immediate thrills of new love) are upsides. And it's far the best for children. Monogamy is so vastly more functional than its alternatives, in so many ways, that it's almost a mystery why it always, across millennia, inspires criticism and hostility—sometimes powerful, sometimes weak, always there. The psychoanalyst Otto Kernberg says that couples in love inspire envy and hostility because their love excludes others. Couples and their social world need each other, but their relationship is like an iffy marriage—always on the ropes.

Doubts about monogamy have seeped into wedding vows. Today self-written vows are as common as traditional ones. Couples choose to write their own because they have doubts about the traditional ones, especially the promises to love, to be faithful, and to stay together until death. Unsure whether they *can* or *will* or even *want to* do those things, they eschew promising in favor of *wishing, hoping*, or *trying* to do them. They also want vows that are unique and heartfelt, in their own style and words. The traditional vows emphasize the couple's free consent to the shape of life that the traditional vows call for, but that shape isn't personal and unique. To choose the traditional ones is to choose to participate in a *shared social pattern* for love and sex lives.

Why Not Just Cohabit?

Widespread skepticism about marriage is one of the legacies of the seventies and eighties, when the back-to-back introductions of the birth control pill and no-fault divorce laws created a divorce epidemic. The pains of those years are still lively cultural memories. They create fear of divorce, hedged marriage vows, and a preference for cohabiting instead of marrying. Many couples believe that the breakup of cohabitation is less traumatic than divorce, but often it isn't, and far more cohabitations break up than marriages.

W. Bradford Wilcox and Laurie DeRose (2017) report that even when the couple have children, cohabitations are much less stable: "Almost half of cohabiting college-educated mothers will break up with their partner before their child turns 12, compared to less than one-fifth of mothers who were married when the child was born." Although Americans tend to think that things are different in Europe, they're not: "Analyzing data from 16 countries across Europe, we find that children born to cohabiting couples are about 90 percent more likely to see their parents break up by the time they turn 12, compared to children born to married parents." In France, that likelihood increased 66 percent; in Norway 88 percent.

The many extant versions of the traditional vows all include the same promises. Every marriage is unique, but the vows do not address their unique qualities because the social world has no stake in intimate, personal aspects of the marriage that don't affect others. The public has a stake only in the *social shape* of marriage, the features of marriage that have social effects and that call for others to behave in certain ways toward the couple. The traditional vows are short and dramatic. Self-written vows tend to be long, as the couple struggle to describe complicated private things that are not really the wedding guests' business.

Of course, the guests, being affectionate friends and relatives, take genuine pleasure in hearing how much the couple mean to each other. But this is the pleasure of an audience at a performance. Promises to share life's adventures or make blueberry muffins, to *listen*, to bring the spouse snacks when they're working late, or any of the other good, sweet, and funny things people promise in self-composed vows—none of these need witnesses and social support, the traditional function of wedding guests. This makes vows, guests, and the wedding itself begin to seem unnecessary. Why put on a big, expensive show, especially if the couple have already been living together for years, as is so often the case today? More and more couples, recognizing this pointlessness, never marry or marry only years later, when they've achieved a nice bank balance. The personal downside of the choice not to marry is the loss to the couple of the protections that formal marriage offers a love relationship. The social downside, when many couples are making this choice, is the weakening of a historic tradition on which many social goods depend.

Traditionally, wedding guests are witnesses who represent all the people who aren't there, so that the society as a whole stands behind this love relationship and becomes a protector of it in whatever ways are appropriate to their connections with the couple— as relatives, close friends, neighbors, legislators, teachers, clergy, doctors, police, and so on. This social recognition is crucial to the stability of the union. The police call the spouse first in the case of an accident. The doctor says different things to the hospitalized patient's mate and to the patient's book-club friend who asks how the patient is doing. Close friends will offer help, advice, and affection, as friends should. The law will give the couple some special tax breaks and legal privileges because by marrying they are doing something good for society.

Has all this, the monogamous heritage of Western cultures, passed its prime? The move toward self-written vows, which so often lay out private, individualistic terms for marriage and are silent about love, fidelity, and permanence, suggests a cultural drift away from it. So do calls to let a thousand love styles bloom—monogamy, serial monogamy, cohabitation, polyamory and other forms of consensual nonmonogamy, and polygamy. Why are love and sex anyone's business but my own? Why is it fine to have three wives or husbands in a row but terrible to have three at the same time—if all parties are agreeable? How is it that the Western world, with its democracies, equality, civil rights, and freedom of speech and religion and press, is still trying to force us all into matrimonial chains? Why not relational freedom?

On the whole, people in the United States, Canada, and most of the Western world enjoy almost absolute relational freedom. No law forbids cohabitation, open marriage, polyamory, or any form of consensual nonmonogamy, and people can live and love as they choose with few exceptions (incestuous relations, in some places first-cousin marriage, relations with children, etc.). But only monogamy is legitimized and favored in law, and only polygamy is legally forbidden. A powerful array of evidence argues that this is just as it should be. By and large, monogamy increases, and polygamy decreases, a society's wealth, freedom, happiness, and stability.

The Perils of Polygamy

In the nineteenth century, Mormon polygamy shocked the American public, and Utah was granted statehood in 1896 only on condition that it prohibit it forever. In 2020, however, Utah decriminalized polygamy, making it something akin to a traffic violation.

There was no outcry, no voices raised questioning whether Utah is meeting its obligation to "prohibit" it. A strong majority of Americans still object to polygamy—80 percent according to a 2020 Gallup poll—but a growing minority regard the majority attitude as prejudice or as outdated prudery. In Canada, a 2018 Ipsos poll found that that 36 percent approved of decriminalizing polygamy.

Those who favor legalization tend to think of polygamy as a lifestyle choice, like cohabitation or consensual nonmonogamy—a question of personal choice. They are also persuaded by a chorus of voices—conservative, liberal, and libertarian—that see the issue in terms of civil rights. These attitudes get reinforced by TV shows that depict lovable, relatable polygamous families and just as often depict monogamy as onerous, miserable, and unnatural.

On Terminology

We call a society polygamous if it permits people to marry plural mates. But, in practice, *polygamy* is always *polygyny*, the marriage of one man to plural wives. *Polyandry*, the marriage of one woman to plural men, is so rare that for all purposes here we can ignore it. (With few exceptions, neither men nor women like it.) Polygamy is illegal in most of the modern societies of the Western world and East Asia, and legal in many African and Middle East nations.

Monogamy, the marriage of two people, is licit and common in all societies. Serial monogamy permits successive monogamous relationships. Strict monogamy forbids divorce

> and makes all marriage permanent. Strict monogamy is not
> the law, but the Roman Catholic Church still requires it.
> *Normative monogamy* is monogamy that is enforced in custom,
> law, or both.

That the entire Western world is formally monogamous is in no small part due to the success of the church in Rome, over many centuries, in enforcing monogamy. Regardless of the church's motives, which in many ways were shrewdly practical, the policy led to a profusion of social benefits. Social scientific studies give persuasive evidence that monogamy predominates in the richest and most powerful nations because monogamy helps make them that way. Monogamy works better than polygamy and outcompetes it. Monogamy explains much of why and how the West achieved its great wealth, advanced science, unmatched power, and great freedoms. Although the reasons why have been told and retold in great detail over the past few decades, they are mostly ignored in popular debates.

Among the fifty wealthiest countries in the world, measured by gross national income per capita, none practices polygamy except seven Middle East states (six of which are oil-rich). Among the fifty poorest nations, *all* permit polygamy except Haiti, and some have high rates of it. The more polygamous a society, the lower its gross domestic product (GDP) per capita. Normative monogamy increases GDP per capita. Monogamous countries are richer even when compared to polygamous societies with similar levels of development.

The fundamental reason why polygyny works less well is what the evolutionary biologist Joseph Henrich calls its "math problem." Boy and girl babies are born in roughly equal numbers. Other things being equal, if some men have plural wives, other men will necessarily have no wives. Here is an illustration of the problem (modeled on Henrich's example). Even when polygyny occurs at what seems like low percentage levels, a surprising number of men are left wifeless. Imagine a very small town, adult population one thousand, with five hundred adult women and five hundred adult men in which only 6 percent of men—thirty—have plural wives. Then suppose ten of them have two wives, eight have three, five have four, four have five, and the remaining three men have, respectively, six, eight, and ten wives. In real-life situations, these are modestly realistic numbers. (Rich and powerful polygynous men often have many more than ten wives. A staggering 40.9 percent of married Nigerian women have a co-wife, compared to a modest 21.6 percent of our hypothetical women in this example.) This adds up to 108 women in polygynous marriages in this small town, and leaves 392 women for 470 men—seventy-eight wifeless men, 15.6 percent of the men. The wifeless men can't go to a neighboring village to find a wife, because polygyny is happening there, too.

Some observers suggest that the shortage of women explains the rise of groups such as the Taliban in Afghanistan, where polygyny "has increased in recent decades, even though the Afghan population has a surplus of men," and Boko Haram, which has kidnapped and raped scores of Nigerian schoolgirls. This excess of deprived men works against peace and prosperity. The unwed men are available to serve as soldiers for powerful men seeking more power, and they commit crimes at higher rates than married men. At the same time, polygynous men have much less time to devote to work and business on account of the high demands on their time and attention of courting and maintaining plural wives and being a father to large numbers of offspring. They can contribute less to the national economies than men in monogamous countries. These combined causes, on a societal level, mean that polygyny results in less peace and political stability, less safety and general social welfare, and less-successful economies. Monogamy results in increased peace, stability, safety, and wealth.

In polygynous societies, to increase the diminished pool of available women, men seek out younger and younger women to marry. The higher the rate of polygyny, the larger the marital age gap grows. Younger wives become very young, poorly educated mothers, and more controllable wives. Early childbearing contributes to poorer mental and physical health—including more depression, nervous breakdowns, and shorter lives than among monogamous women. Polygyny's math problem makes for worse lives for women.

Polygyny sets in motion an unavoidable competition among co-wives for love, companionship, food, clothes, shelter, and, for their children, all those good things plus chances for education and, most important of all, the love, care, and attention of their father. According to a major review of studies on polygyny by Henrich and his colleagues, "Co-wife conflict is ubiquitous in polygynous households. From anthropology, a review of ethnographic data from sixty-nine non-sororal polygynous societies from around the globe reveals no case where co-wife relations could be described as harmonious." Polygynous households have more family breakups, more people moving in and out, more fighting, more violence and abuse of wives—and more abuse, neglect, and violence toward children. Children of polygynous households suffer worse nutrition, worse health, more abuse, and more deaths than those in monogamous households. Does polygyny at least reduce extramarital affairs and divorces as compared to monogamy? No. It leads to as much or more of both. Polygyny is not about love, and does not protect it. All this is one answer to the question why three wives in succession are so much better than three at once.

The more fundamental answer to that question is that monogamy, even serial monogamy, creates no shortage of women. It solves polygyny's math problem: a monogamous man gives up one wife before marrying another. The overall long-term effects—well-studied and -documented—are wealthier, more advanced, more stable, more democratic societies with increased welfare for women and children, equality of men and women, and freedom for everyone. Legalized polygamy makes people less free, not more free.

Love Experiments

With its revolutionary roots and its individualism, the United States has always been friendly to social experiments. In the nineteenth century, there were many of these, pursuing a variety of utopian and religious ideals. The most successful of them, and the sole surviving one, is the extreme form of polygyny introduced in the early 1840s by Joseph Smith and Brigham Young, the founders of the Mormon religion. In the United States and Canada, even though polygamy has always been illegal, it continues to be practiced by tens of thousands of people, usually in connection with religion, and it plays out exactly as it does everywhere else—with an excess of boys (who will be unable to marry due to the shortage of women), child abuse, female subordination, sectarian violence, and sometimes fraught relations with neighboring communities. Once polygamy takes root, it is extremely difficult to dislodge.

Today's fundamentalist Mormon polygamy is still the radical kind that flourished in the mid-nineteenth century, without the limit of four wives that Islam imposes. It encourages men to marry many wives. It has a well-earned dark reputation for child abuse, feud, welfare exploitation, an occasional leader with shocking numbers of wives and children, and more. But it takes the ideal of plural love seriously. As in Islam, men are supposed to love their many wives equally and treat them equally. Mormon fundamentalists consider dyadic love sinful, full of self and pride; men are not supposed to give way to special feeling for a single woman. They may feel a great deal of guilt for being unable to fulfill these imperatives, and, according to the anthropologist William Jankowiak, who writes about them sympathetically, they never do. "Inevitably," he says, "the favorite wife and her children's needs are met first."

North America's other major love experiments in the eighteenth and nineteenth centuries were forms of communitarian life. Some, like the Shakers and the Harmonists, practiced celibacy. The Shakers lasted from the eighteenth century until 1961, when they stopped accepting new members, and the Harmonists from the early nineteenth century until 1905.

The famous Oneida Community in upstate New York survived only from 1848 until 1879. It practiced a form of group marriage and, at least in principle, favored sexual freedom. Group marriage of all with all occurs rarely in world history, and some anthropologists doubt that any system fully deserving the name has ever existed, but Oneida seems to deserve it, unless its short life disqualifies it. Oneida explicitly forbade exclusive love, which it held to be unchristian, and expelled people who married or formed couples who favored each other. Like Mormon polygyny, it deemed romantic love and monogamous marriage selfish and destructive. It, too, had a charismatic, authoritarian leader, John Humphrey Noyes. He taught that what was "natural" was "for all men to love all women, and for all women to love all men." The community demanded that everyone be married to the group, which in practice meant rigid restrictions on having sex. Men and women slept apart. Although everyone was in theory allowed to have sex with anyone (of the opposite sex) who consented, in fact to be allowed to do so they had to first propose a "love interview" via a go-between who would convey one party's proposal to the other and, should it be accepted, would subsequently monitor the pair to be sure no exclusive relationship was developing. The privacy of couples was forbidden and controlled.

Noyes exercised formidable control over every member's sex life. The sex act itself was regulated. Men were not allowed to ejaculate *in sex* or *after sex* unless they had permission to make a baby, and that permission was given sparingly. (Noyes gave himself permission to ejaculate at least nine times—the number that he personally fathered among the community's fifty-eight babies.) Postmenopausal women initiated teenage boys into sex, and older men would do the same for teenage girls. It's a good guess that the custom was more popular among the initiators than among the youth. As one would expect, the system resulted in the sexual initiation of girls as young as ten, though usually immediately after menarche at around thirteen. Noyes undertook most of the initiating of girls himself, but now and then he delegated the privilege to a few of his trusted assistants.

Group and communal experiments enjoyed a revival in the hippie era of the late twentieth century. They typically called for "free sex" or plural love partners yet also imposed tight restrictions on their members' sex lives. Like the Mormons and Oneida, they tended to have charismatic leaders who controlled their followers' sex lives. Kerista, the famous hippie commune from the 1970s, was founded by a man who was convinced by a hallucinatory experience that he was to found a new religion. Kerista practiced "polyfidelity" (and invented the word "compersion" that is now so popular in discussions of and among polyamorists). Kerista forbade members to have children and required men to have vasectomies. It divided people into smaller family groups and allowed them to have sex only with those in their group according to a rotating schedule. They were not asked to have equal feelings for all members, but they were not allowed to enact love by sleeping only or more frequently with their favorite. Like the Oneida Community, Kerista sought to thwart the preferential sexual behavior of monogamous couples who excluded the group, treasured their privacy, and preferred each other.

The satisfactions and freedom that two lovers can enjoy in private intimacy is impossible in groups, which offer at best, as a substitute, friendship, or a loss of individual identity in merger rather than an intensification of individual identity in love. In the group, the individual gets access to plural sexual partners, but not freedom to have sex where, when, and with whom he or she wants. But when intimate coupled love is on offer, it can be hard to resist. The ability of group sex communities to survive depends on how successful they are in banishing coupled love, and success requires a high degree of control over the members' sex lives. If even a small polyamorous group of five or six needs fairly ample lists of rules about who sleeps with whom, when, and being compersionate, larger groups need whole books of them. Kerista at its peak had between thirty and forty members. It lasted two decades, from 1971 to 1991. The Oneida Community lasted for thirty-two years and at its peak had about three hundred members. It ended as Noyes fled in fear of prosecution for statutory rape, and its younger members began to demand exclusive relations in marriage.

Criticism of monogamous marriage reminds me of the old saw about shouting "Fire!" in a crowded theater when there is no fire. Early in the twentieth century, this was not simply an aphorism but a cruel joke that on a number of real-life occasions led to panics and needless deaths in packed halls and theaters. The critics talk about monogamy as a misery-making social fire that must be extinguished. But the evidence on monogamy is in: there's no fire, and people might get hurt scrambling for the exit. From both personal and social points of view, monogamy in marriage based on love is far more likely to work for our good than are any alternatives.

Monogamy is how individuals and their social world cooperate to protect and amplify love. It makes use of every cultural tool available—family life, customs, stories, art, music, learning, ceremony—to create free channels for natural drives to flow and flourish in. It is lovers' best friend. Although not everyone finds or keeps love, everyone benefits when lots of people do. Their loves and marriages keep alive a world where many kinds of rich and fulfilling lives are possible.

Chapter Twelve

MORES AND MANNERS

Dear Miss Manners: I came across this statement on a forum and was wondering what you thought about it: "A host cannot invite a person to a social function without inviting his or her socially recognized partner. It's not permitted by etiquette to only invite half of a couple." Isn't part of entertaining finding a good mix of people to invite? . . .

Gentle Reader: Yes, a host should select interesting guests, and yes, a host cannot invite half of couples to most social events. How are you going to manage doing both?

Miss Manners has a solution for you, but it does not involve making clear to your friends that you can pick interesting people for an evening better than they can for a lifetime.

It is, rather, to make occasions that would be of obvious interest to one but not the other. Luncheon on weekdays is the classic time that partners may be invited separately unless they work together. Or for an activity, such as a fishing expedition, that one practices and the other doesn't . . .

—Judith Martin, *Miss Manners*, May 5, 2011

As more and more couples wed only after living together for years, a new kind of breakup is becoming familiar. Perhaps one or both of the cohabiting couple decides it's time for a baby. Or perhaps one is restless or feels that the relationship "isn't going anywhere." Whatever the reason, they finally decide to marry and have a big wedding with many guests, much finery, and pre- and postceremony rituals and parties, but they divorce before any baby can be out of diapers.

For these couples, the wedding is an end, not a beginning. They probably do not foresee that marriage will make the ground shift under them, and they are thrown off-balance. They may have thought they were already married in the only ways that count and viewed the wedding as a mere formality. Such thinking is usually a mistake. Only getting married makes you married, and getting married almost always changes things, no matter how long a couple have lived together. Of course, most couples are not overthrown by the changes, but enough are to show that weddings make things different.

Among their many purposes, weddings exist to make the couple's withdrawal from the marriage market a public and accepted fact. They change your social identity. Cohabiting does this, too, but much more weakly than a wedding. In weddings, a bevy of mostly single bridesmaids and groomsmen deliver the couple into what is always called the "arms" of matrimony—to bring to mind society's embrace of the couple as a couple. The singles in the wedding party enact the relinquishment of their friend, hoping soon to be relinquished themselves. This not only concretizes their acceptance of the couple's new status but also expresses their hope for a love of their own. It gives—and demands—social validity and respect for the union and establishes their own future right to similar protection. All this helps to ensure that the couple's social group regards the married pair as sexually off-limits, and understands their new mutual dependencies—social, emotional, and economic—and their mutual vulnerabilities and needs.

But the social group is always slightly ambivalent about its members' marriages. It is in favor of the marriage but also feels deserted. Wedding days are usually full of authentic support and affection. After the wedding, however, the couple's family and friends may show some mixed feelings. Parents may cling to their grown children and mutter criticisms of the son- or daughter-in-law. These ambivalences usually die down, but there never comes a time when being part of a couple does not come with a need for negotiating small or large difficulties with friends, families, and acquaintances. It's the stuff that fills agony aunts' columns.

If the social group does not grant the couple respect and valida-tion, it may eventually break them up: third parties may attempt to seduce one of them when the pair have a vulnerable moment; their acquaintances may reject the religion or politics or profession of a new spouse; the larger society may set up social rules or enact laws or create economic incentives that exaggerate conflicts between the partners' individual interests and their interests as a couple. When a couple's social world fails to respect and approve of their marriage, it takes a tough couple to resist outside pressures and hold on to each other. If the social world disapproves of marriage in general, and the couple find its criticisms persuasive, they may approach every stumble in their marriage with a predisposition to believe that it's insurmountable or to interpret it as proof of what people say—that marriage is misery-making.

Married couples signal their status because it is to their advantage that the people around them know that they are married and, often, to whom they are married. Weddings are the most dramatic announcement of the couple's change of status, but weddings are soon over. Afterward, the pair resort to quiet, permanent signals that they are married. One such signal is name changing, but given the breakdown of this custom, it has become a more ambiguous and problematic indication of marital status, and in any case only ever applied to women. Rings are the easiest and best signal because they are gender-neutral and most people everywhere know what a ring on the fourth finger of the left hand means.

If a couple use an obscure social signal, few people will figure out what they are trying to say. In his scholarly history of human marriage, Edward Westermarck reports, "In Easter Island a young married man tattooed the vulva of his wife on his chest as a sign that he was married." In America today, this message would not come through. A couple who get identical heart tattoos on their right wrists instead of wedding rings, or who wear wedding rings on their pinkies, also have failed to give a clear signal.

For millennia, wedding rings, like married names, were only for women. Men's rings became popular in the mid-twentieth century, partly as a result of an advertising campaign by jewelers and the wedding industry that successfully invented a "tradition" of men's rings, and partly because of a change in perception of men's role in marriage, one that included a greater investment in home, family, and domesticity. The new habit is also thought to owe something to lonely soldiers in World War II who wore rings as a symbolic tie to wives at home. In the marriage "fever" that erupted during and after the war, the custom spread until the vast majority of weddings were double-ring ceremonies. A 1947 *Fortune* article titled "Ring Twice" reported that in the late 1930s, only 15 percent of weddings were double-ring ceremonies. By the late 1940s, the figure was approximately 80 percent. Whatever the origins of the custom, it is a happy one.

A marriage is much less necessary to a satisfactory social life than it was a half century ago, and this is a good thing. Those who are unwilling or unable to marry or not yet married should never suffer exclusion for that choice or that situation. Through much of the twentieth century, a man's political and professional career all but required him to be a family man, with a wife and children, and from the 1950s on, a woman past her early twenties without a husband was not invited to many dinners and parties. This was not true in earlier centuries, and perhaps became common in the last half of the twentieth century because marriages became so insecure. The realistic fear of divorce and infidelity meant that social life, for married couples, was socializing with other married people, and spouses moved together in lockstep. As marriage becomes less and less of an indispensable social ticket, spouses are less often called on to do the dreaded spouse dance for their mate's benefit (a fate that still burdens politicians' wives). The ways in which married couples share social life today are much improved.

Married couples usually attend ceremonial occasions together— weddings, funerals, memorial services, and the like. They do not share business meals with their mate's clients, bosses, or colleagues, but when mates are invited to an office social function, of course they attend. If a spouse refuses to bring, or to accompany, their mate to a professional occasion where mates are invited and expected, that, absent special circumstances, may be a breach of marital manners.

Both spouses get invited to social dinners. To invite only one would be interpreted as an insult or even an attack on a marriage. (The usual exceptions include occasions when the other spouse is working out of town, sick, or otherwise unavailable.) A married person, without their spouse, might meet friends of either sex for lunches out. But, with commonsense exceptions, a married hetero-sexual person does not have dinner dates with someone of the spouse's sex and does not *give* dinners, except together with the spouse. In ordinary circumstances, if a married person shows up at a party or social dinner with a date who is not their mate, eyebrows will rise, and other guests will be confused or shocked. There are social groups that do not practice these social habits. Some high-society hosts and hostesses have always ignored them. People whose interests, politics, and professional concerns lead them, or require them, to mix socializing with those interests and concerns also ignore them.

These customs recognize that a spouse is part of a married person's social self, and that people *like and want to be with their husband or wife* on occasions of pleasure. When people fear that a married couple actually don't like each other and don't want to be together, invitations sometimes stop altogether, but even then it's unlikely that anyone will give a solo invitation that challenges the marriage. If a couple separate, they begin to be invited separately to lunch or coffee or to dinner with "just the family." Most hosts are likely to give it a few months before they invite one or the other to larger social occasions, such as a party or dinner other than a family dinner, and then, for another stretch of time, they will be sure to invite *only* one.

Except in special circumstances, no one should ever speak disparagingly to a person about that person's spouse, or criticize the spouse's looks or behavior or make jokes or—especially—sexual remarks about him or her. In *Honor: A History*, the cultural critic James Bowman describes an episode of *The Sopranos* in which one mobster makes a vulgar joke about the physique of another mobster's wife. Johnny, the husband, forms a serious intention to murder the jokester, regarding this as required by honor, despite his friends' and bosses' repeated efforts to talk him out of it. "I want to avenge her honor, as is my right to do . . . Is nothing sacred? I mean this is my wife we're talking about here." For Johnny, Bowman points out, to dishonor his wife is to dishonor him. "I'm making a point! I'm talking about my wife's honor here. My honor." But it's not only Johnny who furiously resents an insult to his mate. All married people do, or if they don't, that is a sign that the marriage is in trouble. Few would resort to murder, but practically all would angrily break off relations or publicly and harshly rebuke the offender. Insult a person's husband or wife and you insult that person. And certainly a person's own mate doesn't make insulting remarks about them to a third party (marriage counselors and clergy excepted). Married couples generally avoid any highly intimate conversations about their marriage with any third party, and definitely do not blackguard their mates in one.

Friends, relatives, and acquaintances of married couples are well aware of how the couple's affections, pride, sense of self and obligation, and overall well-being are tied up with their mates. They instinctively behave as etiquette demands, avoiding gossip about or put-downs of one to the other. Ordinarily, they understand that one mate's illness or disappointment or job problems are deeply upsetting to the other and that the good fortune of one mate is to be congratulated to the other; and so forth. In their interactions with a married person, they are guided by their awareness of that person's ties to their spouse and how those ties create special vulnerabilities. Also, they give each spouse the same level of respect.

Spouses Always Have the Same Status or Rank, Even among Jackdaws

The renowned ethologist Konrad Lorenz reported some remarkable facts about relationships among jackdaws. Jackdaws have an elaborate social hierarchy and are strictly observant of rank, which, once established, does not change. Only once did he observe a "ruling tyrant"—Goldgreen—deposed. Double Aluminum, after an absence of months, returned feeling full of himself, challenged the ruling Goldgreen, and won. This made Double Aluminum the new ruler, and Goldgreen became second-in-command. Double Aluminum soon fell in love with a very low-rank female, and within two days the whole flock knew it. Their marital relationship elevated her to Double Aluminum's own status. Even high-ranking Goldgreen quietly gave way to her at the feeding table when she, by a form of self-display, demanded this. "Since the partners in a jackdaw marriage support each other loyally and bravely in every conflict, and as no pecking order exists between them, they automatically rank as of equal status in their disputes with all other members of the colony; a wife is therefore, of necessity, raised to her husband's position. But the contrary does not hold good—an inviolable law dictates that no male may marry a female that ranks above him," Lorenz wrote in *King Solomon's Ring* (1952).

Jackdaws in this respect are not terribly dissimilar to status-oriented human beings, for whom a woman is elevated by her husband's status, but a man is not elevated by his wife's. It is a double-dyed sort of wrong.

Readers of Anthony Trollope's novels will remember Plantagenet Palliser, later the duke of Omnium. Planty Pall, as he is nicknamed, is upright and courageous but also dull, conventional, rigid, and proud. He married an unconventional, almost wild beauty, Lady Glencora, who loved someone else but was pressed into marriage with this rich and powerful heir to a ducal title. Palliser is often infuriated by Glencora's defiance of the conventions and her gossip-inducing breaches of decorum, but at the same time he stands by her unwaveringly and with such courageous love that we readers, and finally Glencora, too, learn to love him. If Glencora were going to be publicly shamed or ridiculed, Palliser intended to share the shame and ridicule. On one such occasion he announced what in my home we came to

call the Duke of Omnium Principle: In matters affecting reputation, whatever one spouse does, the other does, too. Whatever
one is, the other is. And vice versa. Each places their honor in
the other's hands, sharing the other's social standing, with its
benefits and its exquisite vulnerabilities.

Chapter Thirteen

HAPPY ENDING

So the faithful maiden was married to her sweetheart, Roland. All her grief and pain were over, and only her happiness lay before her. ("Sweetheart Roland")

Then the wedding of the Prince and Briar Rose was celebrated with all Splendor, and they lived happily until they died. ("Briar Rose")

He took her to his kingdom, where he was received with joy, and they lived long and happily together. ("Rapunzel")

—*Grimms' Fairy Tales* (1812–1857)

Weddings are the happy endings in a surprising number of Grimms' fairy tales. The list in this chapter's epigraph is incomplete. It excludes, among others, all those like "Cinderella" and "Snow White and the Seven Dwarfs" in which the wedding is half of the ending and the other half is gruesome punishment for the wrongdoers. But the Grimm brothers were not alone in regarding a wedding as the happiest possible ending. The same is true in a huge proportion of all fiction, great and not great, that ends happily. But it's writers like the Grimms who have given modern cynics their favorite sneer, in which the hopes for marriage and the promises of the wedding vows are dismissed as childish faith in fairy tales.

These critics are right about one thing. Weddings are not endings. In real life, they are typically happy beginnings. Marriage is the founding of a small society that is unique, but the wedding is the ritual celebration of what every marriage shares in common with all other marriages—that here is one more couple who have found love and will build their lives on it. This is good news for them and their world, and it's one of those times in life when it feels better to be like everyone else than to be different. Sometimes being ordinary is the best way to be happy. Sometimes reality, which so often seems to hand out happiness grudgingly, seems to conspire with Mother Nature to be on our side and nudge us into finding some.

People who find a partner in their middle to late twenties to share life with are lucky in many obvious ways. I was not one of the lucky ones. I launched a miserable marriage in my early twenties, and when it ended spent what seemed an eternity being even more miserable. It took years to regain my balance and figure out how to do the very ordinary good thing of finding someone to love and marry.

My postdivorce single life was much like the TV version: horrific working hours as a lawyer, terrible dates and fix-ups, Saturday nights alone with takeout and TV. Then some friends fixed me up with Joe, a psychoanalyst. We quickly abandoned any thought of being anything other than good friends. We took walks, went to the movies, and talked about everything. His ideas, his odd angles on things, got me interested in reading psychoanalytic literature. I had nibbled at this material in graduate school, but now I haunted the psychology shelves in bookstores, trying to understand just why I was living my pale life.

A year or so later, Joe gave a party and invited me. When I showed up, I was slightly taken aback to find myself in a room filled almost entirely with psychoanalysts—a scene I could have imagined only in a Woody Allen movie, back when they were funny. All the psychoanalysts were friendly and warm, but as far as I could tell, the only three people present besides myself who weren't psychoanalysts were Joe's sister; Fred, the husband of Fiona, who was one of the psychoanalysts; and a disgruntled-looking English professor, E. As I learned later, E had been dragged to the party against his will by Fiona and Fred. Fiona and I introduced ourselves and quickly took to each other. After fifteen minutes or so, she looked at me thoughtfully, smiled, and excused herself. I found another psychoanalyst to talk to, but in a few minutes Fiona returned with E in tow and introduced us. E and I exchanged stories about how we happened to be guests at a party of psycho-analysts. He told me that he and Fiona had once been fixed up together, as it happened, like Joe and me, and had become good friends but never lovers. We chatted about the daunting experi-ence of going on a blind date with a psychoanalyst, who might hear everything we said with the profession's famed "third ear." Halfway through the evening, we realized that our intense and exclusive talk, in a party of shrinks, was not going unnoticed. We separated and conscientiously ignored each other for an ineffective twenty minutes.

Six months later, E and I got married. Ours was the first of three marriages spawned at the party. Joe takes credit, but we like to think our example was inspirational. Love was in the air.

When we tried to write our own wedding vows, we didn't like

what we came up with. E then suggested, to my surprise, that we use an archaic Anglican ceremony with all its archaicisms intact (except the one about wifely obedience, which has long since been dropped from almost all American versions, though not from the 1662 Book of Common Prayer). He also suggested we be married by a judge whom a friend recommended. Once again, I took archaic vows before a judge—this one smiling, warm, dignified, and serious all at once—and E and I both willingly pledged our troth. We had read the vows together and loved the graceful, ancient promises, although before the wedding we had felt a bit . . . superior to them. They were "of course," things that were pretty to say but needn't actually be said. This was not at all how it felt when the judge actually asked us the questions and we had to answer them aloud in front of everyone we knew. The judge locked eyes with each of us for a moment as he began to address us, and I found myself meaning the things I was saying from the heart.

Our families and friends, including Joe, Fiona, and Fred, all came to the wedding and wished us well. Mere hours later, when the two of us slipped away from the reception, it seemed to me that all of reality had shifted and that we were new people living in new skins. The experience was not what I would call happy, because it went beyond a good mood or delight; it was higher and wilder. It was also unnerving. I could understand why some people would react negatively to their own weddings; they would mourn the persons they had been and the world they left behind. I was not at all inclined to do that. Unnerved by this new life, yes, but very inclined to be positive about it.

E had nothing but friendly ideas about marriage. He joked about it being a state of high honor, a sort of exclusive club, and would wonder aloud about some annoying married couples, "Who let *them* in?" We lived in a world of people who treated our marriage—all marriages—respectfully. This second marriage was never in doubt. It seemed to right itself almost gyroscopically whenever, inevitably, things tilted wrong. I understood that this was so because the marriage, and its terms, were what we both wanted and because it was what our loving friends wanted for us. Most of them, including Joe, also got married.

Our wedding set in motion a deep consolidation of our relationship, one that I had no idea was coming and had never experienced in my first marriage. Both E and I had to adjust, as almost everyone does, and we were blind to some obvious signs of that adjustment, as almost everyone is. We didn't know it at the time, but the most obvious and absurd sign of this adjustment going on was the eruption of repeated, utterly pointless quibbling. I'll give three examples, but there were many more.

One day, walking the block on 110th Street between Broadway and Amsterdam on Manhattan's Upper West Side, I remarked on how much longer the blocks were up there than those down in the West Seventies. E replied that this was impossible because Broadway and Amsterdam were parallel and, mathematically, the blocks had to be the same length. I responded that since, clearly, they weren't the same length, Amsterdam and Broadway weren't parallel. We actually continued trying to convince each other for the rest of the walk down the block. A second example was bickering, in a supermarket aisle, about whether to get chickpeas or garbanzo beans for our favorite salad. I held out for garbanzos, as I thought they had more flavor, but he preferred chickpeas. I turned a can of garbanzo beans around to study the nutrition label on the back (looking for any scientific support for preferring garbanzos) and discovered that garbanzo beans *were* chickpeas. We laughed hysterically, but we still didn't figure out what the quibbling was all about.

The third example happened in the Park Avenue office of a fertility doctor, whom we visited soon after returning from our honeymoon. We wanted to do everything we could to ensure I got pregnant. The doctor was the happiest and most charming medical man I had ever met, and I was sure that his success rate was so high because just seeing him would make couples' tension instantly dissolve. He began by asking me several ordinary medical questions. I answered no to all of them. E quietly but irritably insisted, after each no, that the true answer was yes. This was very annoying, and the doctor was looking from one to the other of us, puzzled but still cheerful, even more cheerful. He laid down his pen and told me, "I think you're pregnant." He jumped up, grabbed my hand, and pulled me, half running, into the exam room to take my blood. (Faster methods are less reliable very early in pregnancy.) He shook E's hand vigorously as we left, saying, "I hope I never see you again." He called us with the results. I *was* pregnant. "Easiest case I ever had," he crowed, laughing triumphantly. We'll never forget him, but we never saw him again. And our nonsensical, pointless quibbles were also gone forever. Mostly.

Many readers will have seen what was going on here—the need to reassure ourselves of our separate identities, combined with fear of losing this beloved person if *real* anger for real causes should ever erupt. Getting pregnant changed all that. We felt reassured on both fronts, both united and divided by our approaching parenthood. We learned how to have genuine, helpful arguments, and even how to resolve some of them. Many people reach that point more easily than we did, in their own ways.

Intimacy raises the danger of ambivalences and fears and angers. A certain kind of love naturally embraces and contains them. When it is weak or absent, the consequences may be divorce, quarrels laced with murderous anger, attempts at mutual psychic destruction, infidelities, poverty, illness, and the misery of children exposed to these evils. These things are real, and vows and weddings can't prevent them. But that doesn't mean weddings and vows don't help—if you take them seriously and understand them. It doesn't mean that it's safer to shun marriage entirely.

Wedding vows, if they are vows from the heart, made before witnesses you respect and care about, are a potent moment in the ceremony. They change things. The tradition draws power from its brevity, its universality, and its great age, wisdom, and beauty. It deserves respect and protection just as great thousand-year-old works of literature, art, and architecture do. Like them, it remains alive and meaningful, and unlike them, each of us can claim it as our own.

When I found out that I was pregnant so soon after marrying,

I experienced a moment when I could feel a current of time running back to the wedding, back to girlhood, and then forward to a birth and all the other changes that were to come. Dickens describes exactly such a moment in the last words of his novel *Little Dorrit*, where it occurs immediately after a wedding. He leads you away from the wedding ceremony and toward the couple's lives, extending in time, past and future, and in space, social and physical.

> Little Dorrit and her husband walked out of the church alone.
> They paused for a moment on the steps of the portico, looking
> at the fresh perspective of the street in the autumn morning
> sun's bright rays, and then went down.
>
> Went down into a modest life of usefulness and happiness . . .
> They went quietly down into the roaring streets, inseparable and
> blessed; and as they passed along in sunshine and in shade, the
> noisy and the eager, and the arrogant and the froward and the
> vain, fretted, and chafed, and made their usual uproar.

APPENDIX I

Welcome and Prefatory Remarks, Sarum Missal,
Ordo Sponsalia ad Facienda (1506)

We are gathered here, brothers, before God and his angels and all his saints, at the face of the church, to join together two bodies, namely of this man and this woman, *here let the priest look at these persons*, so that they may be one flesh and two souls in the faith and under the laws of God, and at the same time earn everlasting life, no matter what they have done before. I therefore admonish you all that if any of you know any reason why these young people may not lawfully marry, speak up now.

APPENDIX II

Welcome and Prefatory Remarks, Book of Common Prayer,
Solemnizacion of Matrimonie (1549)

At the day appointed for Solemnizacion of matrimonie, the persones to be married shal come into the bodie of the churche, with
theyr frendes and neighbors. And there the priest shal thus saye.

Deerely beloved frendes, we are gathered together here in the
syght of God, and in the face of his congregacion, to joyne together
this man and this woman in holy matrimonie, which is an honorable estate instituted of God in paradise, in the time of mannes
innocencie, signifying unto us the misticall union that is betwixte
Christe and his Churche: whiche holy estate, Christe adorned and
beutified with his presence, and first miracle that he wrought in
Cana of Galile, and is commended of Sainct Paule to be honourable
emong all men; and therefore is not to bee enterprised, nor taken in
hande unadvisedlye, lightelye, or wantonly, to satisfie mens carnal
lustes and appetites, like brute beastes that have no understanding:
but reverentely, discretely, advisedly, soberly, and in the feare of
God. Duely consideryng the causes for the whiche matrimonie was
ordeined. One cause was the procreacion of children, to be brought
up in the feare and nurture of the Lord, and prayse of God. Secondly it was ordeined for a remedie agaynst sinne, and to avoide
fornicacion, that suche persones as bee maried, might live chastlie

in matrimonie, and kepe themselves undefiled membres of Christes bodye. Thirdelye for the mutuall societie, helpe, and coumfort, that the one oughte to have of thother, both in prosperitie and adversitie. Into the whiche holy estate these two persones present: come nowe to be joyned. Therefore if any man can shewe any juste cause why they maie not lawfully be joyned so together: Leat him now speake, or els hereafter for ever hold his peace.

APPENDIX III

*Sarum and Book of Common Prayer,
Consents and Vows Compared*

Salient differences are marked in bold.

1506 Sarum Consent (Trans. from Latin)	1549 Book of Common Prayer Consent
Groom *N.*, Will you have this woman as your wife, to love, honor, hold, and keep her, in health and in sickness, **as a husband should a wife**, and forsaking all others for her, keep only to her, so long as you both shall live?	Groom *N.*, Wilte thou have this woman to thy **wedded** wife, to live together **after Goddes ordeinaunce in the holy estate of matrimonie**. Wilt thou love her, coumforte her, honor, and kepe her in sicknesse and in health? And forsaking all other kepe thee only to her, so long as you both shall live?
Bride *N.*, Will you have this man as your husband, to obey and serve him; and love, honor, and keep him in health and sickness, **as a wife should a husband**, and, forsaking all others for him, keep only to him, so long as you both shall live?	Bride *N.*, Wilt thou have this man to thy **wedded** houseband, to live together **after Goddes ordeinaunce, in the holy estate of matrimonie**? Wilt thou obey him, and serve him, love, honor, and kepe him in sickenes and in health? And forsaking al other kepe thee onely to him, so long as you bothe shall live?

1506 Sarum Vows (Marrying Sentences)	1549 Book of Common Prayer Vows (Marrying Sentences)
Groom I, *N.*, take the, *N.*, to my wedded wif, to haue and to holde fro this day forward, for bettere for wers, for richer for pouerer, in sykenesse and in hele; tyl dethe vs departe, **if holy church it woll ordeyne**, and therto y plight the my trouthe.	Groom I *N.* take thee *N.* to my wedded wife, to have and to holde from this day forwarde, for better, for wurse, for richer, for poorer, in sickenes, and in health, **to love and to cherishe**, til death us departe: **according to Goddes holy ordeinaunce**: And therto I plight thee my trouth.
Bride I, *N.*, take the, *N.*, to my wedded housbonde, to haue and to holde fro this day forwarde, for better for worse, for richer for pouerer, in sykenesse and in hele, to be bonere and buxum in bedde and atte borde, tyll dethe vs departhe, **if holy churche it woll ordeyne**, and therto I plight the my trouthe.	Bride I *N.* take thee *N.* to my wedded husbande, to have and to holde from this day forwarde, for better, for woorse, for richer, for poorer, in sickenes and in health, **to love, cherishe, and to obey**, till death us departe: accordyng to **Goddes holy ordeinaunce**: And thereto I geve thee my trouth.

1506 Sarum Groom's Solo Speech	1552 Book of Common Prayer Groom's Solo Speech
With this rynge I the wed, **and this gold and siluer I the geue**, and with my bodi I the worshipe, and with all my worldely catel I thee endowe.	With this ring I thee wed: with my body I thee worship, and with all my worldly goodes I thee endow. *(In 1549, this speech was the same as in the Sarum rite.)*

APPENDIX IV

To Have and to Hold:
The Poetics of Binomials in the Wedding Vows

The ancient phrase "to have and to hold" is one of the more mysterious ones in the old rite. It occurs as early as the fourteenth century in the Sarum rite and elsewhere, but not everywhere. The words have a strong legal flavor, but there is a scholarly debate that points to other, nonlegal flavors. The phrase is not a vow and makes no promise. The "have" seems to be the plain "have" of *relationship*. If you marry, you *have* a mate in the same sense that you have a brother or a friend or a lawyer. Among the many meanings of "hold" at the time were to keep, preserve, or retain, and also to keep in being. So "to have and to hold from this day forward" means "to have and retain." (This and all other examples and definitions in this appendix come from the *Oxford English Dictionary* unless otherwise noted.) It simply restates the fact of the marriage and its permanence. The rest of the marrying sentence gives vows about the obligations of marriage.

Other glosses are plausible, too. Both words also had, and have, *sexual* meanings. In a York manuscript of 1403, but not in Sarum's rite, this was made almost, but not quite, explicit: "Here I take ye to my wedded [wyfe/housband], to hald and to haue at bed and at borde fro this day forwarde . . ." Then as now, to "have" someone was to have sex with that person; to "hold" was to embrace. "Hold" then also meant to guard, preserve from harm, uphold, or support, but when "hold" is coupled with "have," these other meanings are merely overtones.

"To have and to hold" is what linguists call a "binomial" expression, a phrase with two words that are customarily joined in a customary meaning. (On this subject, refer to Ursula Schaefer's essay on "to have and to hold," cited in the Note on Sources for chapter 3 at the end of this book.) They may use alliteration, rhythm, or rhyme so as to be "catchy," as grammarist.com says. "To have and to hold" is alliterative, rhythmic, and so catchy that it has survived for nine or ten centuries, in and out of the wedding vows. Binomials intensify meaning, and in an oral culture function as aids to memory. Many are "one-way": you can't reverse their order without breaking their meaning. You can't say "white and black" and retain the meaning of the binomial "black and white." Moods are up and down but not down and up.

"To have and to hold" was a binomial long before it appeared in fourteenth-century wedding rites. "Have now and hold" (Hafa nu ond geheald) is in *Beowulf*, which first appears in writing around 1000 CE and was composed much earlier. A tenth-century translation of Bede's Latin "ad tenenda seruandaque" into Old English gives it as "to habbanne & to healdenne." The Sarum vows in a fourteenth-century rite contain a remarkably long string of binomials: "to hau and to holden . . . for bettere for wers, for richere for porere, in seknesse and in helthe to be boneyre and buxsum in bedde and at borde"—a total of six binomials in the woman's vow.

The repetition of binomials is not accidental but stylistic. It is how an oral culture builds a structure of words, a familiar formula, that taps feelings and inspires respect and understanding—all at once. It leaves no ambiguities about what the couple meant. It beautifies and dignifies their act by making it poetry.

CREDITS

ACKNOWLEDGMENTS

Many people contributed to the birth and growth of this book, with learning, questions, corrections, stories, warm support, and curiosity that reached into corners I had neglected. My debt to Robert Messenger is beyond estimation. His fine judgment combined with risk-tolerant intelligence, along with unfailing taste and a bottomless fund of enthusiasm, contributed hugely to any merit the book might claim. I am indebted to many others at Simon & Schuster, especially Isabel Casares and Rachael DeShano, who always knew the answers. Michael Carlisle supported this project from its outset and guided it into the world with his usual combination of literary acumen and savoir faire.

Anne Vance's suggestions on an early draft were invaluable. Eleanor Johnson's lively comments on the medieval sections were enormously helpful and a delight in themselves. Benjamin Saltzman shared his knowledge of Old English. Zoë Pollak's careful and sympathetic comments guided me in both stets and cuts. I benefited from a lecture by Fr. Michael Hilbert, S.J. on church influences in the history of marriage. Every writer should have a friendly reader as wise about ideas and craft as Thomas Filbin. And what don't I owe to the contributions of the Barnard and Columbia students who attended my 2015 philosophy class on marriage, which was not only eye-opening and enlightening for me but also tremendous fun?

ACKNOWLEDGMENTS

I owe thanks to the British Library and especially to its reference librarians who located the misshelved copy of a slender booklet, aged about ninety years, that contained a remarkable quotation, not only for the find but also for sharing my joy and mini-triumph and even—beyond what duty required—helping me to scan it.

Thanks to W. Bradford Wilcox and Alysse ElHage for all their own contributions to understanding marriage in the contemporary world and for their generous help.

Then there are James Mendelson and Julia Teal Reynolds, who, throughout the writing years, read chapters and told stories and shared insights that have added an invisible spice to the flavor of the book.

As for Edward Mendelson—he is the book. He also is responsible for suggesting three quotations, two epigraphs, and one story.

NOTE ON SOURCES

Novels and stories, written and spoken, are my most important sources. Some are named in the preceding pages but you will find almost none in this note, which includes mostly scholarly and journalistic works. From *Little Women* in my girlhood to *Wolf Hall* last year, novels have taught me about love and marriage in a way that only personal experience rivals. Fiction's risk-free encounters with imagined worlds reach deep enough to change us—without wrecking our lives. Scholarly sources greatly enrich, but can't replace, what we learn from real life and great literature.

Chapter 1: My *Troth*?

Scholarly sources include Michael M. Sheehan, "Theory and Practice: Marriage of the Unfree and Poor in Medieval Society" (1988), in *Marriage, Family, and Law in Medieval Europe: Collected Studies*, ed. James K. Farge (1997); David Herlihy, "Biology and History: The Triumph of Monogamy," *Journal of Interdisciplinary History* (1995); and, here and throughout this book, Edward Westermarck's monumental and still unsurpassed *The History of Human Marriage* (1891; 5th edition, 1922).

Chapter 2: Promises

See Thomas Aquinas, "On Vows" in his *Summa Theologica*, Second Part of the Second Part, Question 88, especially Article 7. Daniel Donoghue's account of Wulfstan is in his *Old English Literature: A Short Introduction* (2004); Donoghue quotes Wulfstan's sermon from Henry Sweet, *An Anglo-Saxon Reader in Prose and Verse* (1876). On the word "forswear," see the *Oxford English Dictionary*, which points out secondary meanings that have accrued to the word; for example, to abandon, forsake, or give up things other than a promise or the truth. Auden's introduction appears in Joseph Jacobs, *The Pied Piper and Other Tales* (1963). Chief among my sources on promises is Herbert Schlesinger's wonderfully wise *Promises, Oaths, and Vows: On the Psychology of Promising* (2008). On John Calvin's view of marriage as a covenant in which God is a third party, see John Witte Jr. and Joel A. Nichols, "More Than a Mere Contract: Marriage as Contract and Covenant in Law and Theology," *University of St. Thomas Law Journal* (2008). See also Witte's *From Sacrament to Contract: Marriage, Religion, and Law in the Western Tradition* (1997). For a subtle and entertaining essay on the ins and outs of vows and their binding qualities, see David Schalkwyk, "Shakespeare's Speech," *Journal of Medieval and Early Modern Studies* (2010). Objections to marriage vows as "barbarities" date back more than a century and a half; see, for example, Gail Hamilton's denunciation in *A New Atmosphere* (1870). Much-debated biblical statements about vows and oaths include Exodus 20:7, Deuteronomy 5:11, and (discussed in Schlesinger) Matthew 5:33–38.

On the psychological effect of vows and promises and the episode of the fainting bridegroom, see Thomas Cooper, "'Wilt Thou Have This Woman?' Asking God's Blessing on Consenting Adults," in *Anglican Marriage Rites: A Symposium*, ed. Kenneth W. Stevenson (2011); Patricia Kanngiesser et al., "Keeping Them Honest: Promises Reduce Cheating in Adolescents," *Journal of Behavioral Decision Making* (2020); Nicolas Jacquemet et al., "Truth Telling under Oath," *Management Science* (2019); Mark K. Rutgers, "Will the Phoenix Fly Again? Reflections on the Efficacy of Oaths as a Means to Secure Honesty," *Review of Social Economy* (2013); Stephen A. Buetow and Peter Adams, "Oath-Taking: A Divine Prescription for Health-Related Behaviour Change?" *Medical Hypotheses* (2010); and Mark L. Dean, "Effects of Vow-Making on Adherence to a 12-Week Personal Fitness Program," PhD diss., Louisville, KY, 2001.

Chapter 3: The Evolution of the Marriage Vows

In this chapter I have relied on a wide range of historical works and scholarly editions.

The principal historical works include: F. L. Ganshof, *Feudalism*, trans. Philip Grierson (1964); Harold J. Berman, *Law and Revolution: The Formation of the Western Legal Tradition* (1983); Patrick Wormald, *The Making of English Law: King Alfred to the Twelfth Century* (1999); Samuel Cardwell, *"Be wifmannes beweddunge*: Betrothals and Weddings in Anglo-Saxon England," *Anglo-Saxon England* (2022); R. H. Helmholz, "Marriage Contracts in Medieval England," in *To Have and to Hold: Marrying and Its Documentation in Western Christendom, 400–1600,* ed. Philip L. Reynolds and John Witte Jr. (2007); Sarah Larratt Keefer, "Manuals," in *The Liturgical Books of Anglo-Saxon England,* ed. Richard W. Pfaff and John Witte Jr. (1995); Karl Joseph Heidecker, *The Divorce of Lothar II: Christian Marriage and Political Power in the Carolingian World,* trans. Tanis M. Guest (2010); J. Wickham Legg, *On the Retention of the Word* Obey *in the Marriage Service of the Book of Common Prayer* (1915); Jean-Baptiste Molin and Protais Mutembe, *Le Rituel du Mariage en France du XIIe au XVIe Siècle* (1974); Helen Gittos, *Liturgy, Architecture, and Sacred Places in Anglo-Saxon England* (2013); Conor McCarthy, *Marriage in Medieval England: Law, Literature and Practice* (2004); Antoine Villien, *The History and Liturgy, of the Sacraments,* trans. H. W. Edwards (1932); Kenneth W. Stevenson, *Nuptial Blessing: A Study of Christian Marriage Rites* (1982); Sir Frederick Pollock and Frederic William Maitland, *The History of English Law before the Time of Edward I* (1895); *A Cultural History of Marriage in the Medieval Age,* ed. Joanne M. Ferraro and Frederik Pedersen, vol. 2 (1988).

Also: Brucia Witthoft, "Marriage Rituals and Marriage Chests in Quattrocento Florence," *Artibus et Historiae* (1982); Francis C. Eeles,

On a Fifteenth-Century York Missal Formerly Used at Broughton-in-Amounderness, Lancashire (1935); and John Thrupp, *The Anglo-Saxon Home: A History of the Domestic Institutions and Customs of England, from the Fifth to the Eleventh Century* (1862). For long views and big pictures, I referred to many works, including Lawrence Stone, *The Family, Sex, and Marriage in England 1500–1800* (1979); David Herlihy, *Medieval Households* (1985); Jack Goody, *The Development of the Family and Marriage in Europe* (1983); Philip L. Reynolds, *How Marriage Became One of the Sacraments: The Sacramental Theology of Marriage from Its Medieval Origins to the Council of Trent* (2016); and John Witte Jr., "Marriage Contracts, Liturgies, and Properties in Reformation Geneva," in *To Have and To Hold*, ed. Reynolds and Witte (cited above).

The translations of the Anglo-Saxon fealty oath and *Be Wifmannes Beweddung* are from *Ancient Laws and Institutes of England: Comprising Laws Enacted under the Anglo-Saxon Kings from Aethelbirht to Cnut*, vol. 1, ed. Benjamin Thorpe (1840). The Anglo-Saxon marriage contract is from *English Historical Documents, Volume I, c. 500–1042*, ed. Dorothy Whitelock (1979). The Anglo-Saxon poems "The Wife's Lament" and "The Husband's Message" are from *A Choice of Anglo-Saxon Verse*, ed. Richard Hamer (2015). The scholarly edition of the York manual, *Manuale et Processionale ad Usum Insignis Ecclesiae Eboracensis*, ed. W. G. Henderson (Surtees Society, 1875), was so useful that my first copy fell apart and my second copy is seriously at risk. This volume includes not only the York manual but excerpts from many others, including the Sarum manual, the matrimonial ceremonies from the Hereford and Welsh manuals, and the Magdalen Pontifical. I have also made intensive use of *The Sarum Missal: Edited from Three Early Manuscripts*, ed. J. Wickham Legg (1916); and *The Pontifical of Magdalen College*, ed. H. A. Wilson (1910). Further sources include Edmundo Martène, *De Antiquis Ecclesiae Ritibus Libri Tres* (1763); Galbert de Bruges, *Histoire du Meurtre de Charles Le Bon, Comte de Flandre*, ed. Henri Pirenne (1891); Dirk Schultze, "English Portions of the Marriage Ordo in Manuscripts of German Provenance," *Anglia* (2022); Ursula Schaefer, "On the Linguistic and Social Development of a Binomial:

The Example of *to have and to hold*," in *Binomials in the History of English*, ed. Joanna Kopaczyk and Hans Sauer (2017); Mark Searle and Kenneth W. Stevenson, *Documents of the Marriage Liturgy* (1992); and Conor McCarthy's introduction to *Love, Sex, and Marriage in the Middle Ages: A Sourcebook* (2004). I have relied gratefully throughout this chapter on the vast resources of the *Oxford English Dictionary*.

Chapter 4: How Thomas Cranmer Brought Love to Marriage

Historical sources for this chapter include Diarmaid MacCulloch's two biographies, *Thomas Cranmer: A Life* (1996, rev. 2017) and *Thomas Cromwell: A Revolutionary Life* (2018). Also Nancy Basler Bjorklund, "'A Godly Wyfe Is an Helper': Matthew Parker and the Defense of Clerical Marriage," *Sixteenth Century Journal* (2003). Of the works cited above in the note to chapter 3, I have relied especially on those by Francis C. Eeles, J. Wickham Legg, Jean-Baptiste Molin and Protais Mutembe, Dirk Schultze, and Ursula Schaefer, as well as W. G. Henderson's edition of the York manual for the Surtees Society. I have again relied gratefully throughout this chapter on the *Oxford English Dictionary*.

Chapter 5: A Brief Biography of Love

Sample wedding vows are everywhere on the internet; my examples are from the website of the Association of Civil Marriage Celebrants of Victoria Incorporated (acmcv.org.au); Young, Hip, & Married (younghipandmarried .com); and Heart of Sidona Weddings (heartofsedonaweddings.com). The quotation from *Faust* is from David Luke's translation of *Faust Part I* (1987). Other sources for this chapter include the National Marriage Project, *The State of Our Unions: Marriage in America* (2012); Geoffrey F. Miller, "Sexual Selection for Moral Virtues," *Quarterly Review of Biology* (2007); Jeremy Holmes, "Sense and Sensibility: Hedonic Intersubjectivity and the Erotic

Imagination," in *Attachment and Sexuality*, ed. Diana Diamond et al. (2007); Donatella Marazzati and Domenico Canale, "Hormonal Changes When Falling in Love," *Psychoneuroendocrinology* (2004); Philip Shaver and Cindy Hazan, "Being Lonely, Falling in Love: Perspectives from Attachment Theory," *Journal of Social Behavior and Personality* (1987); Arthur Aron et al., "Falling in Love: Prospective Studies of Self-Concept Change," *Journal of Personality and Social Psychology* (1995).

Chapter 6: A Mutual Admiration Society

The versions of the marriage rite quoted in this chapter derive largely from works already cited in chapter 3: *The Sarum Missal: Edited from Three Early Manuscripts*, ed. J. Wickham Legg (1916); *The Pontifical of Magdalen College*, ed. H. A. Wilson (1910); and the text and appendixes in the edition of the York Missal *Manuale et Processionale ad Usum Insignis Ecclesiae Eboracensis*, ed. W. G. Henderson (Surtees Society, 1875). The *Oxford English Dictionary* was again indispensable. The story about Jane Eyre and St. John Rivers comes, of course, from Charlotte Brontë's *Jane Eyre* (1847). The American omission of "with my body" is discussed in Isaac Candler, *A Summary View of America* (1824). The still well-known song line is from "You Made Me Love You (I Didn't Want to Do It)," composed more than a century ago, in 1913, by James V. Monaco, with lyrics by Joseph McCarthy.

Chapter 7: On Our Own: Love and Law

Legal cases, including *McGuire v. McGuire*, may be found in *Modern Family Law: Cases and Materials*, ed. D. Kelly Weisberg and Susan Frelich Appleton (2010). Among many cases that I consulted are *Orr v. Orr*, 440 U.S. 268 (1979); *Medical Center of Vermont v. Lorrain*, 165 Vt. 12 (1996); *Connor v. Southwest Florida Regional Center*, 668 So. 2d 175 (FLA 1995); *Medical Business Associates v. Steiner*, 183 A.D.2d 86 (N.Y. App. Div. 1992); *Heller v. Somdahl et al.*, 206 N.C.

App. 313 (N.C. Ct. App. 2010); and *Hutelmyer v. Cox*, 133 N.C. App. 364 (N.C. Ct. App. 1999). This chapter also refers to the Texas Family Code, Sec. 2.501, Duty to Support; California Family Code, 4300–4303, Duty to Support; Illinois Compiled Statutes 750 ILCS 65, Rights of Married Persons Act, and 740 ILCS 5/1, Illinois Alienation of Affections Act; and other state laws, including those described in Brian Bix, *The Oxford Introductions to U.S. Law: Family Law* (2013). On "heart balm," see Jill Jones, "Fanning an Old Flame: Alienation of Affections and Criminal Conversation Revisited," *Pepperdine Law Review* (1998). For views sympathetic to the plight of a woman betrayed, see also Joanna L. Grossman and Lawrence Friedman, *Inside the Castle: Law and the Family in 20th Century America* (2011).

Chapter 8: No Matter What

On medieval wedding rites, see the citations for chapter 3 to the York and Sarum missals, the Magdalen Pontifical, the Westminster rite, and the 1915 essay by J. Wickham Legg; also the *Oxford English Dictionary*. The Latin phrase from a York rite was quoted in Eeles, cited in chapter 3.

Modern sources for this chapter include William L. Roberts, "Significant Elements in the Relationship of Long-Married Couples," *International Journal of Aging and Human Development* (1980); Frank D. Fincham and Ross W. May, "Infidelity in Romantic Relationships," *Current Opinion in Psychology* (2017); Laura Betzig, "Causes of Conjugal Dissolution: A Cross-Cultural Study," *Current Anthropology* (1989); Menelaos Apostolou et al., "Reasons That Could Lead People to Divorce in an Evolutionary Perspective: Evidence from Cyprus," *Journal of Divorce & Remarriage* (2019); Jeffrey Winking and Jeremy Koster, "Timing, Initiators, and Causes of Divorce in a Mayangna/Miskito Community in Nicaragua," *Social Sciences* (2021); Shelby B. Scott et al., "Reasons for Divorce and Recollections of Premarital Intervention: Implications for Improving Relationship Education," *Couple and Family Psychology* (2013). I have again learned much from the *Oxford English Dictionary*.

On abandonment during a partner's illness, see Michael J. Glantz et al., "Gender Disparity in the Rate of Partner Abandonment in Patients with Serious Medical Illness," *Cancer* (2009); Laurel L. Northouse et al., "The Impact of Caregiving on the Psychological Well-Being of Family Caregivers and Cancer Patients," *Seminars in Oncology Nursing* (2012); Anna-Leila Williams and Ruth McCorkle, "Cancer Family Caregivers during the Palliative, Hospice, and Bereavement Phases: A Review of the Descriptive Psychosocial Literature," *Palliative & Supportive Care* (2011); and Stephen R. Shuchter and Sidney Zisook, "The Course of Normal Grief," in *Handbook of Bereavement*, ed. Margaret S. Stroebe et al. (1993).

Virginia Woolf's diary entry is from August 2, 1926. For an instructive study of the rule of three, with a rich set of examples, see Patrick Barry, "The Rule of Three," *Legal Communication & Rhetoric* (2018).

The concluding quotation is from Tom Coughlin, "Nothing Could Prepare Me for Watching My Wife Slip Away," *New York Times*, August 24, 2021.

Chapter 9: Fidelity and Its Discontents

Online sources for this chapter include: Megan Brenan, "Americans Say Birth Control, Divorce Most 'Morally Acceptable,'" Gallup News, June 9, 2022; Alan J. Hawkins and Heather Smith, "National Survey Reveals Generational Differences in Consensual Non-monogamy," Institute for Family Studies, September 11, 2019; Wendy Wang, "Who Cheats More? The Demographics of Infidelity in America," Institute for Family Studies, January 10, 2018; Christy Bieber, "Revealing Divorce Statistics in 2023," Forbes Advisor, August 8, 2023.

I also consulted Laura Betzig's "Causes of Conjugal Dissolution: A Cross-Cultural Study," cited in chapter 8; Judith Wallerstein and Sandra Blakeslee, *The Good Marriage: How and Why Love Lasts* (1995); Leon J. Saul, *Fidelity and Infidelity and What Makes or Breaks a Marriage* (1967); Lydia G. Roos et al., "Post-traumatic Stress and Psychological Health following Infidelity in Unmarried Young Adults," *Stress and Health* (2019); Man Cheung Chung et al., "Self-Esteem, Personality and Post Traumatic Stress Symptoms following the Dissolution of a Dating Relationship," *Stress and Health* (2002); Frank M. Dattilio, "Extramarital Affairs: The Much-Overlooked PTSD," *Behavior Therapist* (2004); Frank W. Weathers and Terence M. Keane, "The Criterion A Problem Revisited: Controversies and Challenges in Defining and Measuring Psychological Trauma," *Journal of Traumatic Stress* (2007).

Studies of the effects of infidelity on mortality and health include: Theodore F. Robles et al., "Marital Quality and Health: A Meta-analytic Review," *Psychological Bulletin* (2014); Mark A. Whisman et al., "Marital Satisfaction and Mortality in the United States Adult Population," *Health Psychology* (2018); and Jamila Bookwala and Trent Gaugler, "Relationship Quality and 5-Year Mortality Risk," *Health Psychology* (2020). Also: Elaine D. Eaker et al., "Marital Status, Marital Strain, and Risk of Coronary Heart Disease or Total Mortality: The Framingham Offspring Study," *Psychosomatic Medicine* (2007); Brenton Boyd and Tia Solh, "Takotsubo Cardiomyopathy: Review of Broken Heart Syndrome," *JAAPA* (2020); M. R. Shrout, "The Health Consequences of Stress in Couples: A Review and New Integrated Dyadic Biobehavioral Stress Model," *Brain, Behavior, and Immunity—Health* (2021); Kristina Orth-Gomér et al., "Marital Stress Worsens Prognosis in Women with Coronary Heart Disease: The Stockholm Female Coronary Risk Study," *JAMA* (2000); Michael J. Rohrbaugh et al., "Effect of Marital Quality on Eight-Year Survival of Patients with Heart Failure," *American Journal of Cardiology* (2006); Janice K. Kiecolt-Glaser et al., "The Gut Reaction to Couples' Relationship Troubles: A Route to Gut Dysbiosis through Changes in Depressive Symptoms," *Psychoneuroendocrinology* (2021).

And also: Sarah C. E. Stanton et al., "Perceived Partner Responsiveness, Daily Negative Affect Reactivity, and All-Cause Mortality: A 20-Year Longitudinal Study," *Psychosomatic Medicine* (2019); Benjamin

Warach and Lawrence Josephs, "The Aftershocks of Infidelity: A Review of Infidelity-Based Attachment Trauma," *Sexual and Relationship Therapy* (2021); B. Burman and G. Margolin, "Analysis of the Association between Marital Relationships and Health Problems: An Interactional Perspective," *Psychological Bulletin* (1992); Janice K. Kiecolt-Glaser and Stephanie J. Wilson, "Lovesick: How Couples' Relationships Influence Health," *Annual Review of Clinical Psychology* (2017); Martin Daly and Margo I. Wilson, "The Evolutionary Psychology of Marriage and Divorce," in *The Ties That Bind: Perspectives on Marriage and Cohabitation*, ed. Linda J. Waite et al. (2000); Annmarie Caño and K. Daniel O'Leary, "Infidelity and Separations Precipitate Major Depressive Episodes and Symptoms of Nonspecific Depression and Anxiety," *Journal of Consulting and Clinical Psychology* (2000); A. D. Fisher et al., "Stable Extramarital Affairs Are Breaking the Heart," *International Journal of Andrology* (2012); Richard A. Stein, "Cardiovascular Response to Sexual Activity," *American Journal of Cardiology* (2000).

See also studies by Frank S. Pittman III, including *Private Lies: Infidelity and the Betrayal of Intimacy* (1989); "Teaching Fidelity," *Journal of Clinical Psychology* (2005); and "The Relationship, if Any, between Marriage and Infidelity," *Journal of Couple and Relationship Therapy* (2005).

My quotation from *The Odyssey* is from Robert Fitzgerald's translation (1961). Bertrand Russell denounced monogamy in *Marriage and Morals* (1929) and recanted in his *Autobiography* (vol. 3, 1969). See Ray Monk, *Bertrand Russell: The Ghost of Madness, 1921–1970* (2000), and Alan Ryan, *Bertrand Russell: A Political Life* (1988).

On polyamory and its rules, see Michael Castleman, "Why Many Long-Term Polyamorous Couples Thrive," *Psychology Today*, October 16, 2021; Aryelle Siclait, "8 Rules You Should Be Following if You're in a Polyamorous Relationship," *Women's Health*, September 7, 2019; Forrest Hangen et al., "Delineating the Boundaries between Nonmonogamy and Infidelity: Bringing Consent Back into Definitions of Consensual Nonmonogamy with Latent Profile Analysis," *Journal of Sex Research* (2019).

For both surprising new angles and venerable truths about love, see Otto Kernberg, *Love Relations: Normality and Pathology* (1995).

Chapter 10: Love against Death

References to early texts are taken from sources already cited for chapter 3, especially the edition of the Magdalen Pontifical; the excerpts from a fifteenth-century Welsh manual in the Surtees Society edition of the York manual; Sarum and York missals quoted in the 1915 essay by J. Wickham Legg; and the study of the early fifteenth-century York Missal by Francis C. Eeles. I quote from David Raeburn's translation of Ovid's *Metamorphoses* (2002) and again from Robert Fitzgerald's translation of Homer's *Odyssey*.

Chapter 11: Love and Monogamy: The World They Make

As in chapter 9, I have consulted Otto Kernberg, *Love Relations: Normality and Pathology* (1995). On cohabitation, I refer to W. Bradford Wilcox and Laurie DeRose, "In Europe, Cohabitation Is Stable . . . Right?" Brookings, March 27, 2017.

On arguments for legalizing polygamy, see Fredrik deBoer, "It's Time to Legalize Polygamy: Why Group Marriage Is the Next Horizon of Social Liberalism," Politico, June 26, 2015; Jillian Keenan, "Legalize Polygamy! No. I Am Not Kidding," Slate, April 15, 2013; and Tony Perkins, "'Time Has Arrived' to Legalize Polygamy, Writes New York Judge," Daily Signal, October 4, 2022.

Richard H. Thaler and Cass Sunstein, in *Nudge: Improving Decisions About Health, Wealth, and Happiness* (2008), argue for deregulating marriage. Christopher Ryan and Cacilda Jethá, authors of *Sex at Dawn: How We Mate, Why We Stray, and What It Means for Modern Relationships* (2010), regard exclusive relationships as misery-making. David Barash and Judith Eve Lipton, in

NOTE ON SOURCES

The Myth of Monogamy: Fidelity and Infidelity in Animals and People (2001), argue that polygamy is the natural human mating system.

Tolerant or sympathetic attitudes toward polygamy are defended in Martha Nussbaum, *Liberty of Conscience: In Defense of America's Tradition of Religious Equality* (2008); Andrew F. March, "Is There a Right to Polygamy? Marriage, Equality and Subsidizing Families in Liberal Public Justification," *Journal of Moral Philosophy* (2011); and Miriam Koktvedgaard Zeitzen, *Polygamy: A Cross-Cultural Analysis* (2008).

This chapter's statistics and other data on polygamy call on many sources, and lean most heavily on Joseph Henrich et al., "The Puzzle of Monogamous Marriage," *Philosophical Transactions of the Royal Society* (2012) and Henrich's book *The WEIRDest People in the World: How the West Became Psychologically Peculiar and Particularly Prosperous* (2020). See also the decision in the Canadian reference case *Reference re: Section 293 of the Criminal Code in Canada* (2011). On the social and economic effects of polygamy as a social system, see also the essay by David Herlihy cited in the note to chapter 1; Michèle Tertilt, "Polygyny, Fertility, and Savings," *Journal of Political Economy* (2005); Michèle Tertilt, "Polygyny, Women's Rights, and Development," *Journal of the European Economic Association* (2010); "Afghanistan: Marriage," Landinfo, May 19, 2011; Max Planck Institute for Foreign Private Law and Private International Law, "Family Structure and Family Law in Afghanistan: A Report of the Fact-Finding Mission to Afghanistan," January–March 2005; Matt Ridley, "More Monogamy Makes the World Less Violent," *Times* (London), December 22, 2014; Alean Al-Krenawi and John R. Graham, "A Comparison of Family Functioning, Life and Marital Satisfaction, and Mental Health of Women in Polygamous and Monogamous Marriages," *International Journal of Social Psychiatry* (2006); Gilles Saint-Paul, "Genes, Legitimacy and Hypergamy: Another Look at the Economics of Marriage," Birkbeck College and IZA, Discussion Paper No. 4456, September 2009; and Ronald Cohen, "Brittle Marriage as a Stable System: The Kanuri Case," in *Divorce and After*, ed. Paul Bohannan

(1971). The statistic on Nigerian polygyny is from Youssef Courbage and Emmanuel Todd, *A Convergence of Civilizations: The Transformation of Muslim Societies around the World* (2011).

On the Oneida and other communities, see William Smith, *Families and Communes: An Examination of Nontraditional Lifestyles* (1999); *Free Love in Utopia: John Humphrey Noyes and the Origin of the Oneida Community*, comp. George Wallingford Noyes (2001); Timothy Miller, *The 60s Communes: Hippies and Beyond* (1999); Leander Kahney, "Free Love and Selling Macs," *Wired*, April 23, 2002; Michael Cummings, "A Tale of Two Communes: A Scholar and His Errors," in Fellowship for International Community, *Communities Directory: A Guide to Cooperative Living* (2nd ed., 1995); and C. Allyn Russell, "The Rise and Decline of the Shakers," *New York History*, January 1998.

Chapter 12: Mores and Manners

Edward Westermarck reports on the chest tattoo in his *History of Human Marriage*, cited in the note to chapter 1. On men's wedding rings, see Vicki Howard, "A 'Real Man's Ring': Gender and the Invention of Tradition," *Journal of Social History* (2003). On honor, see James Bowman, *Honor: A History* (2006).

INDEX

ABOUT THE AUTHOR

Cheryl Mendelson is a Harvard Law School graduate, a sometime philosophy professor, and a novelist (*Morningside Heights* and *Love, Work, Children*). In 1999, she authored the classic bestselling resource for every American household *Home Comforts*. Born into a rural family in Greene County, Pennsylvania, she lives in New York City with her husband.